LIFE
BEYOND
DEATH

Also by Collective Healing Anonymous

Collective Healing Anonymous Basics

www.discoverCHA.org

Collective Healing Anonymous
in collaboration with Peace President

LIFE
BEYOND
DEATH

The Ego's Journey of Being Human

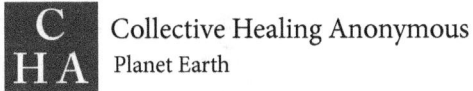
Collective Healing Anonymous
Planet Earth

Collective Healing Anonymous
Planet Earth

© 2024 Collective Healing Anonymous

All rights reserved. No part of this book may be reproduced in any manner without the written permission from the author and publisher.

ISBN 978-0-9862276-4-6

Contents

PART ONE
Toward Understanding Ego Consciousness
0

The CHA Dedication i

Introduction iii

1 Beyond Introductions 1
2 The Basic Life Pattern of Every Human Being 5
3 Biological Beginnings: The Foundation of Experience 15
4 Instinctual Drives: Primal Forces of Biological Survival 19
5 The Emergence of Mind 23
6 The Mystery of Identification: Universal Awareness as the Body-Mind Complex 27
7 The Ego's Dependence on Primal Instincts: Foundations of the False Self 29
8 Recap: Primal Forces as Tools of the Ego 37
9 The Second Fundamental Instinct: Repetition as Security 39
10 The Ego's Collective Survival: Seeking Like-Minded Egos and Belief Systems 43
11 The Divisive Nature of Ego: Inner Conflict and Outer Division 47
12 Key Ingredients to Waking Up from the Trance 51
13 You Are Awareness, Presence 55
14 How Do I Know if the Ego is Running My Life? 59
15 Transitioning to a Deeper Understanding of Awakening 63

PART TWO
Toward Realizing Ultimate Reality Herenow
65

16 Practical Aspects of Awakening 67
17 Exploring the Trance of Separation 73
18 Reclaiming Attention: A Deeper Understanding of the Trance 79
19 Self-Honesty: The Key to Waking Up and Freedom from Suffering 83
20 The Mystery of Life: Understanding the Two Basic Aspects of Existence 87
21 The Hidden Suffering of Misidentification: How the Egoic Self Breeds Fear and False Beliefs 93
22 A Deeper Look at the Illusion of Separation 99
23 The Path to Liberation: Realizing the True Self Beyond Illusion 105
24 Egoic Tricks: How the Ego Hijacks Spirituality 111
25 The Survival System and Awareness: Navigating Human Existence 117
26 The Ultimate Freedom: Surrendering the Egoic Self to Universal Intelligence 123
27 Realizing the Ultimate Truth: Trusting the Unknown 129

APPENDIX
133

I   Ego: A Creation of the Nervous System 133
II   About Collective Healing Anonymous (CHA) 139
III   The Foundational Themes of CHA 141
IV   The 12 Steps of Collective Healing Anonymous 143
V   The Essence of the Peace President Collection of Books 145

The CHA Dedication

Collective Healing Anonymous (CHA) is a loving invitation and compassionate opportunity to be deeply honest with ourselves through a revolutionary non-religious, yet highly spiritual, Twelve Step Process toward healing, feeling, and awakening. As we begin realizing our primal innocence and truth of ourselves through this journey of self-love, forgiveness, and acceptance, we rediscover our natural wholeness and worthiness that never left. By sincerely acknowledging and healing whatever obsessions, compulsions, addictions, and identity challenges holding us back from living a life of everlasting inner freedom and joyful peacefulness, we reclaim autonomy of our body and mind. As willing and grateful participants of CHA and Life, we dedicate ourselves to genuine inner transformation, peaceful coexistence, and Self-Realization—Enlightenment.

Introduction

Life Beyond Death: The Ego's Journey of Being Human explores the profound transformation from living through the limited lens of ego consciousness to awakening to our true nature as pure awareness. The book is structured in two parts: the first part delves into understanding the nature of the ego and how it forms a psychological self or "personal identity" that dominates much of human experience, often creating suffering and limiting our potential. The second part shifts focus, guiding readers toward freedom from the egoic mind by illuminating a path and opportunity to awaken to the boundless awareness within—our truest nature, sometimes referred to as Cosmic Consciousness, God, Unconditional Universal Intelligence, or Reality.

The nature of the ego is complex and multifaceted. In traditional psychology, the ego is often seen as the mediator between our basic desires and our moral conscience, helping us navigate the external world. Philosophically, the ego can be viewed as a mental construct formed by our thoughts, beliefs, and memories. In spirituality, however, the ego is often considered an illusion—a false self that separates us from our inherent unity with the universe—as the Universe. The ego does not exist as a concrete entity; rather, it is a product of streaming mental energies like thought, constantly seeking control, validation, and attachment to maintain its sense of "self." Understanding this illusory and fleeting nature of mind allows us to move beyond the limitations of living ego-driven lives and begin to live from a place of authenticity and presence, herenow.

Introduction

Throughout history, people have found guidance through sacred practices that help them transcend egoic consciousness and realize their true nature—Enlightenment or Self-Realization. Practices like meditation, yoga, self-inquiry, nature immersion, and centering prayer allow us to quiet the mind and turn inward, shedding the layers of conditioning that obscure our essence. Meditation, for example, invites us to witness our thoughts and sensations without attachment, revealing the impermanent nature of all experience, and of course, the apparent egoic self. Yoga harmonizes body and mind promoting balance and self-awareness. Self-inquiry sets a trajectory for investigating if thoughts or beliefs are in fact absolutely true, or are we operating unconsciously and reactively. Ultimately, self-inquiry asks the essential question, "Who am I?" peeling away the false layers of identity constructed by the ego—as egoic mind. Nature immersion reconnects us to a sense of wonder and interconnectedness with all that is, and centering prayer offers the opportunity to wholeheartedly consent to divine action as the divine presence within, creating a silent communion with our own consciousness. Each of these practices guides us to let go of egoic control, allowing life to flow naturally with ease, balance, and grace.

However, regardless of the scientific, religious, spiritual, or philosophical traditions one may follow, practice, or identify with, there is a single common denominator: awareness. Awareness is the essential, liberating force that makes all experience possible. Without awareness, there would be no perception, understanding, or life as we know it. Awareness is the foundation that allows each of us to experience reality, to grow, to learn, and ultimately, to awaken.

This book also provides practical steps for awakening and self-liberation through these practices, encouraging readers to willingly, openly, earnestly, and sincerley become aware; and to observe, question, and release egoic energies dominating their lives.

In the appendix, readers will find information about the authors—Collective Healing Anonymous and Peace President—as well as 12 empowering steps for healing, feeling, and awakening, along with foundational themes created by Collective Healing Anonymous.

As you journey through these pages, may you find not only an understanding of the ego's journey of an apparent existence and death, but also the inspiration to awaken to a life of profound freedom, peace, and unity with all that is.

Part 1

Toward Understanding Ego Consciousness

*How Biological Survival Turns into
Psychological Survival*

Open and allow healing, feeling, and
~ Awakening ~

— Chapter 1 —

Beyond Introductions

Preamble: The Power of Repetition

You may notice, as you journey through this book, a certain redundancy in the ideas presented—concepts and themes that seem to be revisited, restated, and explored from multiple angles. This is not accidental, nor is it a result of over-explanation. Rather, it is intentional and essential to the process of awakening and self-realization.

The mind, conditioned over many years by beliefs, ideas, and societal programming, is deeply entrenched in its patterns of thinking and perceiving. These mental grooves—our habitual ways of understanding ourselves and the world—often run so deep that it takes repetition and a variety of perspectives to begin loosening their hold. By revisiting core ideas again and again, from different angles, we create the opportunity for these old patterns to soften, dissolve, and eventually be replaced by the clarity of true insight.

This book is not merely about understanding concepts intellectually; it is about transforming how we experience life. And just as with any form of reconditioning, the mind requires repeated exposure to the truth in order to break free from its long-standing illusions. Each chapter, each idea, is like a subtle turn of the wheel, helping to deepen your recognition of the universal truth beyond the personal mind.

It is in this spirit of patience and persistence that the teachings in this book are presented. Allow the repetition to sink in, to chip away at the layers of conditioning, and to guide you deeper into the direct experience of your true nature. What may seem redundant is, in fact, a powerful tool for liberation.

Awakening from the Dream and Trance of Separation

For most of us, life unfolds within the boundaries of the egoic self—the part of the mind that constantly reinforces a sense of separation between "me" and "the world." From the moment we are born, we are conditioned to see ourselves as individuals, distinct and apart from others, living in a world of concepts, identities, and roles. We are taught to strive for success, accumulate knowledge, and define our worth based on external achievements, appearances, and self-concepts and images. In this way, we become trapped in a mental trance—a conditioned and programmed dream that mentally and emotionally veils our true nature.

But beneath this dream lies a profound and liberating truth: the essence of who we are is not the body, not the mind, not the story of "me," but something infinitely deeper—universal awareness. This universal intelligence is the timeless, formless ground of all existence, the source from which everything arises and into which everything dissolves. Some call this mysterious force God or Cosmic Consciousness or Universal Intelligence or Source Essence of All Creation. Regardless of what the indescribable Mystery is labeled, it is the silent witness behind every thought, feeling, and experience. It is the one reality that remains constant and unchanging, even as we witness our body-mind complex and the world around us constantly shifting and changing.

The content of this book serves as a guide to waking up from the illusion of separation and remembering the oneness that we have always been. Drawing from ancient and modern-day spiritual wisdom, contemporary Psychology and practical examples, we explore how the egoic mind creates the illusion of a personal self and how this illusion can be dissolved. We examine the universal journey of the human experience—how we first develop a sense of individuality (ego) and then transcend it (egolessness), discovering that we are, in fact, the infinite awareness that was never born and can never die.

Throughout this book, we delve into the timeless truths that have been spoken by enlightened masters throughout history. Whether referred to as God-realization, Self-realization, Enlightenment, or by any other name, the core message remains the same: the realization of our inseparable and eternal nature is the key to true freedom, unconditional happiness, and boundless everlasting love. This possibility is not an intellectual understanding but a direct, lived experience that transforms how we see ourselves and the world.

Beyond Introductions

As you journey through these pages, you will come to understand that the universal is playing through all life forms, both animate and inanimate. In religious terms, it is as though God is playing a game of hide and seek with itself, creating the illusion of separation through the egoic mind, only to provide the opportunity for it to awaken to the truth of inseparable oneness. This is the plight and potential of the human experience—to first become immersed in the dream of egohood or personhood, gathering skills and identity along the way, and then to transcend those limitations by awakening to the infinite, formless grace that has always been present within.

What lies ahead is an exploration of how the mind—composed of intellect, memory, imagination, and the ego—creates a false sense of "I" (or me-ness) that leads to suffering. We will investigate how, through sacred processes like meditation, yoga, and self-inquiry, we can dissolve these illusions and allow the deeper universal intelligence to guide our lives.

Ultimately, this book reveals how the true nature of existence is unconditional happiness and love, not bound by the limitations of the psychological self or personal identity, but freely available to us when we recognize that we *are* that happiness, we *are* that love.

This journey is about awakening to the reality that the universe is alive within us. Rather, what appears as the body-mind complex or "you" is arising from the real Universal You. It is about realizing that beneath every experience, every thought, and every emotion, there is a deeper, timeless awareness—a universal intelligence that is always present, always peaceful, and always free—the REAL YOUniverse.

As you turn these pages, know that the journey we are embarking on is NOT about becoming something new or attaining some higher state. It is about the recognition or revelation of who we truly are herenow—beyond the experience of the mind, beyond the experience of the body, and beyond all fleeting experiences of life—the timeless, formless, infinite, unchanging truth of our being. It is about realizing the source of all things, the place where there is no birth, no death, only the timeless presence of being itself—herenow. Pure Awareness. And in the hereness of now, you will discover that you are already free and always have been, unbounded, complete, enough. You are already whole. You are already the universal awareness that you have been seeking.

Welcome to the journey of healing, feeling, awakening.

Welcome to *Life beyond Death*.
The Ego's Journey of Being Human.

— Chapter 2 —

The Basic Life Pattern of Every Human Being

This chapter outlines the basic life pattern shared by all humans, from instinct-driven survival to spiritual awakening. It describes the stages of conditioning, identity formation, questioning, and inner transformation, ultimately guiding individuals toward rediscovering their true nature as universal awareness beyond the egoic self.

The life pattern of every human being follows a common trajectory, often without awareness, and can be broken down into distinct phases. Each stage represents a deeper experience of the self, the world, and ultimately, the discovery of what it means to live in alignment with true awareness (as awareness)—rather than through programmed filters or conditioned patterns of the egoic mind operating as the mental survival system. Understanding this process is essential to awakening from the trance of separation and finding true fulfillment.

It begins with the experience of the physical form, where our initial awareness is rooted in our bodily sensations and survival instincts arising from the primative brain. As infants, we experience the world primarily through the body—hunger, comfort, warmth, and safety. The body as an abstracted creation of the nervous system. (See Appendix I—Ego: A Creation of the Nervous System.) Slowly, as we develop, we enter into the second phase, the experience of the mind, where we begin to form thoughts, memories, and personal identity based on our interactions with the world.

At some point in this developmental process, we become entranced—identified with the body-mind complex. This is where the sense of being a separate "me" (ego) arises, and from here, much of our life is driven by the ego's need for validation, survival, and control. Thus, identifying as ego, we search for a lasting sense of happiness, safety, and worthiness in the external world—in relationships, achievements, social roles, and material possessions. However, as time passes, some people begin to realize their life is suffering, how they have been reliving and repeating reactive and unconscious patterns of dissatisfaction. This suffering often illuminates their entire life is actually an ongoing identity crisis, the ego's journey of confusion and ill content. And, when the individual questions their value, purpose, or place in the world, resistance usually thwarts the process of waking up; thus, the personal ego continues to seek fulfillment externally, rather than seeking their infinite source of happiness within.

For example, someone may spend years chasing career success, believing that the next promotion or financial milestone will finally bring the happiness and security they seek. Yet, after each achievement, there is a fleeting sense of satisfaction, followed by the familiar feeling of incompleteness. Similarly, others may find themselves stuck in codependent relationships, hoping that external love or validation will provide them with the worthiness they cannot find within. Often, when the dissatisfaction becomes so great, this thought arises, "There must be another way to live!" The individual may even move from one relationship to another, thinking that the "right" partner will fill the void or pangs of unworthiness, only to discover the insufferable and debilitating cycle repeating. Whether it be seeking fulfillment in money, behaviors, social media, jobs, religion, mood altering substances, another person, and so forth, that pattern is almost the entire nature of any and all addictive thoughts, emotions, and behaviors.

At this stage of waking up when painful patterns no longer work, individuals face a crucial choice: to either continue the loop of looking for love in all the wrong places, or to begin questioning it. For those who begin to question this endless cycle, a new phase emerges—what is commonly referred to as the spiritual path.

The Spiritual Path: Questioning the Loop

On the spiritual path, the individual begins to question not only their actions but all of their beliefs about themselves, others, life, the world, and even the nature of reality or God. This marks a profound shift from looking outward for happiness and fulfillment to turning inward in search of the source of happiness and inner serenity—the true-SELF. This phase involves challenging the assumptions, identities, behaviors, and roles that the person has unconsciously adopted throughout life, habits that were conditioned by family, society, and culture.

Fundamentally speaking, the spiritual path leads to the realization that life, as it unfolds for practically everyone on the planet, can be characterized by seven phases: Pre-programming, Individuation, Programming, Deprogramming, Reprogramming, Disidentification, and Surrender.

Stage 1 - Pre-programming

Life begins with pre-programming, where we operate largely from primative instincts, proclivities, and tendencies hardwired for survival in our biological memory. These primal forces govern our earliest experiences. For example, as infants, we cry when hungry or uncomfortable and instinctively seek comfort and nourishment. These automatic responses are our most basic tools for survival, acting without conscious thought or deliberate action. As we grow, these tendencies evolve but remain centered on seeking pleasure and avoiding pain, rooted in the body's survival mechanisms.

Stage 2 - Individuation

The second stage is the process of individuation by which pure, inseparable Universal Awareness becomes identified with a specific, separate form—as a unique body-mind complex. This is the moment when awareness, which is always inseparable and universal, seemingly condenses into a single, defined point of focus (individuated awareness): thereby establishing a seemingly real yet illusory "me." In this process, the individual (an individuated awareness), starts to perceive themselves as separate from others and the world around them, which sustains the greatly limited egoic survival perspective and process of self-preservation that the egoic mind thrives on; because it is rooted in animalistic competition that is naturally divisive, internally.

As we increasingly identify with our body, sensations, feelings, thoughts, and experience, individuation marks the beginning of the ego's emergence and habits of sustaining itself, as the false entirety of who we are. In fact, ego or egoic mind is nothing more than fleeting mental energies that do not have any power except when identified with. For example, a child starts to recognize their name, their preferences, and their ability to control objects in their environment, all of which reinforce the belief in being a separate self. This sense of individuation and personal identity (psychological self) strengthens as we grow older, shaping how we relate to the world. However, despite the arising of ego consciousness through Individuation and all of its self-made problems, inner conflict, and external divisions it creates when identified with it, this process is a natural and necessary part of human development; thereby allowing us to navigate the world as seemingly separate beings; all the while wielding pure potential to discover the inseparable reality of ourselves, the source of all existence.

Stage 3 - Programming

Once we have individuated, we enter the stage of programming, where society, family, and culture begin to shape our beliefs, behaviors, and identity more intensely than during the first two stages. We are taught to believe opinions and interpretations of what is right and wrong, how to behave, and what roles we are expected to play in life. This stage molds our thought patterns, emotions, self-image and self-concept based upon someone else's unconscious programming, conditioning, and false sense of self. That is why most generational patterns either harmful or helpful, continue to be passed down; beliefs and behaviors that seem nearly impossible to break or change, because what we believe, say, and do has been so deeply ingrained in our psyche since day one. Most, if not all of these habits primarily go unquestioned, consciously.

For example, someone raised in a family that values success through hard work might be conditioned to believe that their worth is directly tied to their achievements. Similarly, cultural expectations about gender, social roles, or religion can heavily influence the way a person thinks about themselves and the world. This phase of programming is largely unconscious, as we absorb beliefs and expectations from our surroundings, shaping the egoic identity(s) we carry into adulthood. These are egoic identities that ego will protect and defend at all costs; even if it means death of the body.

Stage 4 - Deprogramming

The fourth stage is deprogramming, which begins when we start to wake up to the fact that our family programming and social and cultural conditioning have shaped our thoughts and behaviors, and not necessarily for our overall well-being or the greater good. And are NOT who or what one essentially is. This is the point where we begin to question the beliefs, reactions, and behaviors we have been unconsciously programmed to follow, noticing how automatic patterns often drive our thoughts and actions, creating and sustaining suffering. Suffering as worry, anxiety, identity confusion, fear, stress, greed, self-hatred, and so on.

For example, someone who has always believed that financial success equals self-worth may start to ask, "Why am I never truly satisfied and feel secure, no matter how much money I make?" This is a key moment of realization, as we start to see how much of our life has been governed by survival instincts, societal conditioning, and false beliefs. Deprogramming allows us to break away from these influences and recognize that the happiness, security, worthiness, and fulfillment we seek externally cannot truly satisfy us in the long term.

Stage 5 - Reprogramming

After deprogramming, the next phase is reprogramming, where we consciously choose to let go of outdated beliefs and behaviors and replace them with new, healthier ones. This stage involves conscious decision-making and the intentional reshaping of thought patterns to reflect inner truth rather than societal or ego-driven influences.

For example, someone might begin practicing mindfulness or yoga to stop reacting automatically to stress, or they may choose to embrace self-love instead of self-hate or constantly seeking approval from others. Reprogramming involves actively noticing and releasing patterns like those of self-judgment that no longer serve us, and replacing them with thoughts, behaviors, and practices that align with our deeper awareness and self-love. This phase marks a period of self-empowerment, where we take control of our inner world and redirect it toward inner growth, maturity, and truth. This stage also marks the conscious decision to reclaim control and autonomy over our body and mind, recognizing that we have allowed the ego-mind to chaotically distort our thinking and dictate our actions.

Stage 6 - Disidentification

Disidentification marks a profound shift in the spiritual journey, where we begin to see through the illusion that we are solely the body, mind, or ego. In this stage, we consciously detach from the identities and roles that have dominated our lives and recognize that they do not define our true essence. This process is about unraveling the identification with thoughts, beliefs, memories, emotions, behaviors, body images, sensations, identities, and roles that we have taken on throughout our lives.

In disidentification, we start to realize that we are not the thoughts we think, the roles we play, identities we believe we are, the feelings and sensations we feel, or the experiences we have—we are the awareness in which all of these things occur. This does not mean we reject the body or the mind, but rather, we stop seeing them as the source of who we are. For example, someone may have spent their entire life identifying with their career, believing that their job title defines their value. In disidentification, they realize that while the career is part of their life, it does not define their essence or worth.

This stage is about witnessing the mind's activities without being caught up in them, without identifying as them. When thoughts of fear, judgment, or inadequacy arise, we observe them but no longer identify with them as "me." Rather than saying "I am a bad person." or "I am not good enough." we would say, "The mind is saying it is a bad person." or "The mind believes it is not good enough." By creating this distance between what is you and what is not you, we move beyond the grip of the ego and its need to control, defend, rationalize, or justify. Instead, we experience a deeper sense of freedom and inner expansion as we no longer react to life's circumstances from the limited perspective of the ego; those stressful and conflicted energies of survival, protection, and defense.

Through disidentification, we begin to live more fully from a place of awareness and fearlessness rather than claiming that our thoughts define us, where the external circumstances of life, whether positive or negative, no longer shake our inner sense of peace and clarity and everlasting sense of self. This stage brings a profound inner shift, where we stop living from the trance of separation and instead, experience life from the perspective of witnessing awareness, beyond the confines of the ego.

Stage 7 - Surrender

The final stage is surrender, where we release the need to control or manage our lives through the ego's lens. In this phase, we recognize that there is a deeper intelligence—a transparent universal awareness—that can guide our life far more effectively than our egoic mind. Surrender does not mean giving up; it means giving up, absolutely. And, in a pragmatic way, it means letting go of the ego's desire to control every outcome by trusting the natural flow of life.

In this stage, we allow universal transparent intelligence to lead the way, instead of relying on our ego-based fears, desires, and expectations. For instance, someone who has spent years trying to control their career path might finally release the need to control every step, trusting that life will unfold as it inevitably does. This surrender brings profound inner peace, as we stop fighting against life and begin to align our trust with it. In this stage, we become clear that thoughts hold no absolute truth and therefore become only noise in the background of experience. We recognize that we are not separate from the whole, and in that recognition, we experience true freedom and fulfillment as universal transparent awareness itSELF—the Source of All Existence—Reality—pure unconditional love.

How Most People Are Stuck in Arrested Development: The Programming Stage

For many, the programming stage becomes an unintentional destination rather than a stepping stone on the journey of conscious evolution. In this phase, we unconsciously adopt the beliefs, values, and behaviors imparted to us by family, society, and culture, forming a mental script that we play out on repeat. While this stage is natural and necessary for early development, most people become stuck in a state of arrested development here, unconsciously looping through the same ideas, beliefs, and reactions as if they are fixed truths. This creates a repetitive cycle, where thought patterns become mental habits, and behaviors are re-enacted mindlessly, without awareness.

For example, someone raised with the belief that who they are is only defined by their religious customs or cultural heritage and often spend a lifetime chasing external validation without ever questioning if these values resonate with their deeper self. Similarly, a person taught to avoid conflict may repeatedly fall into people-pleasing behaviors, sacrificing their own needs and boundaries to maintain approval from others. Additionally, someone born into a culture or nation where war and military dominance are normalized may never realize that a significant part of their egoic identity is rooted in these maladaptive collective beliefs—beliefs that inherently resist true peaceful coexistence. Over time, these programmed beliefs and behaviors harden into rigid habits, reinforcing the ego's sense of control and predictability beyond our awareness, until we begin looking inwardly.

This arrested development is the ego's playground—a space where it can maintain its dominance over our thoughts and actions, both individually and collectively as cultural groups, families, or nations. The ego clings to familiar patterns because they offer a sense of security and stability, however limited or unfulfilling. For the ego, change is a threat, and any potential shift towards deeper awareness or transformation is met with resistance. Moving beyond programming into stages like deprogramming or reprogramming requires inner growth and change, yet the ego cannot thrive in change or in the presence of conscious, self-directed transformation.

In this way, arrested development keeps us in a state of complacency, continually reinforcing the ego's identity and limitations. By looping through the same beliefs and reactions, we unknowingly surrender our potential to live conscious, authentic lives. To move forward, we must consciously recognize and question our programmed patterns, breaking free from the ego's grip and opening ourselves to the possibility of inner transformation and true growth.

Recognizing our arrested development in the programming stage brings us to a crucial crossroads: the need to question the very beliefs and behaviors that have kept us confined. However, when we begin to question our programming, it can feel unsettling, almost as if we are dissociating from ourselves or our experiences. This feeling often arises because we are so deeply identified with our conditioned responses that stepping back from those comfortable patterns feels foreign or disorienting. Yet, what we may not realize is that we have already been dissociated or fragmented by unconsciously aligning with the ego's narratives and external expectations, which separate us from our authentic self. This disconnection is why suffering feels so embedded in our lives; it has become normalized, though it is not our natural state.

To wake up from this trance of ego, however, does not mean dissociating further. Instead, it means learning to disidentify from the ego's constructs without disconnecting from our present experience. True awakening involves seeing through the illusion of egoic identity while remaining fully present and aware, allowing us to reconnect with a deeper sense of peace and authenticity.

The Difference Between Dissociation and Dis-identification

While dissociation and dis-identification might seem similar on the surface, they are fundamentally different processes with very distinct psychological and spiritual implications.

Dissociation is a psychological defense mechanism often associated with avoidance, denial, or escape from uncomfortable experiences, like the experiencing of difficult feelings, painful thoughts, or negative emotions. When someone dissociates, they create a mental separation from reality in an attempt to disconnect from their experience, from the environment, or even their own body. This often happens as a response to trauma or overwhelming stress, where the mind distances itself as a way of coping with pain or fear. In fact, most people on the planet are living in a dissociated egoic state and unaware that this chronic dissociation process is stuck in a loop. It isn't until an acute episode of dissociation comes into awareness that one senses there are underlying patterns controlling them. For instance, the feeling and habit of numbing through coping mechanisms or addictions, which indicate they are detached, as if they are not fully present to their experience. In short, dissociation is a reactive state where the mind cuts off from the full experience of the self or situation to avoid discomfort.

On the other hand, dis-identification is a conscious and mindful process of recognizing that we are not the roles, thoughts, emotions, actions, or external identities that we once believed defined us. Dis-identification does not involve avoidance or denial but instead involves awareness. It is the deliberate practice of observing the mind's patterns and body's behaviors—such as emotions, thoughts, and external identities—without becoming attached or defined by them. When we dis-identify from the egoic mind, we are not escaping from reality but rather stepping back from the illusion that our thoughts and behaviors or roles are who we truly are.

For example, if someone feels anger, dissociation might lead them to shut down, ignore the emotion, or deny that they are upset. In contrast, dis-identification would allow the person to acknowledge the anger, observe it without judgment, and understand that while anger is a present emotion, it does not define their essence or true-self. Dis-identification allows for a deeper connection to awareness and presence, while dissociation fragments or veils our true experience.

In essence, dissociation is a retreat from reality, while dis-identification is an act of freeing oneself from the limitations of ego and reclaiming awareness and okayness of all experiencing. One disconnects us from the present moment; the other empowers us to see beyond the mind and its attachments, fostering a deeper connection to our true nature. Which do you prefer?

End of Chapter Wisdom

Though the details may vary from person to person, the overall structure of the human journey from instinct-driven survival to spiritual awakening remains consistent. This seven-stage process—pre-programming, individuation, programming, deprogramming, reprogramming, disidentification, and surrender—guides us from conditioned behavior to the discovery of our true nature as universal awareness. Most people remain trapped in the early stages, seeking fulfillment through external means and unaware that their true-self lies beneath these conditioned patterns and is infinitely all pervasive.

However, those who begin to question these patterns and their fleeting sense of self often embark on a path of spiritual awakening, where they rediscover the wholeness and inner freedom that transcend the egoic mind and the illusory separation that the body-mind complex projects. Although stages are seemingly necessary, in surrender, we begin realizing the only True-Self there ever was—the inseparable timeless YOUniverse that has always been herenow.

— Chapter 3 —

Biological Beginnings: The Foundation of Experience

This chapter focuses on the idea that the beginning of the experience of life is purely biological, responding as primal mental faculties with negligible involvement from higher mental or psychological processes until later on in the evolution of consciousness and personal development.

At the beginning of human life, survival is fundamentally about the body's primary and absolute instinct to avoid discomfort and seek comfort, responding automatically to physical sensations without any conscious thought or analysis. This is rooted in biological and physiological processes, much like any other animal; often called the reptilian brain. During this phase, the body is governed by primal instincts, with no involvement from higher mental functions or psychological awareness. This period is devoid of psychological complexities, governed solely by the body's automatic responses to its environment. At birth, the infant is entirely dependent on its biological needs being met, continuing the process that began in the womb.

Prior to the brain's development of sophisticated interpretations, motivations, or abstractions, there is no internal dialogue, no conscious thought, or meaningful psychological processes. The nervous system is functioning at a primal level, reacting to sensations of discomfort—such as hunger or temperature changes—and triggering physical responses to address those needs. There is no planning, strategizing, or mental processing involved in this stage of existence. The body simply reacts based upon primative mental faculties.

For instance, the primary drive of an infant is to avoid painful or uncomfortable sensations, such as hunger pangs or fluctuation in temperature (hot and cold), and to alleviate them by instinctual means, such as crying. The infant does not consciously seek to be fed or warmed; instead, the nervous system triggers these actions to maintain balance and ensure survival. This is biological survival at its core, devoid of mental participation.

Initially, the body continues to rely on the same life-support system it had inside the womb. While still in the mother's uterus, the developing fetus receives nutrients automatically through the umbilical cord connected to the mother's body which acts as an incubator. There was no effort required to seek nourishment or safety—these were provided passively through biological processes. This unbroken chain of biological support continues after birth, with one major difference: the severing of the umbilical cord.

The cutting of the cord marks a significant shift in how survival is maintained. No longer passively connected to the mother's body, the newborn must now engage the external environment in a new way, though still without conscious intent. The infant relies on the surrounding environment—primarily the mother or other caretakers to meet its survival needs. Yet, these interactions remain firmly grounded in biology. The body of the infant continues to operate on instinctual responses, driven by the need to maintain homeostasis, physiological balance.

This transition signals the beginning of a gradual process, where biological needs and environmental interactions lay the groundwork for what will later become psychological survival. However, at this point in the infant's life, survival is purely a matter of the body reacting to its needs, driven by primal, physiological mechanisms. There is no "mind" at play yet, no sense of self-preservation, only the body ensuring that the fundamental requirements for survival are met.

End of Chapter Wisdom

At the core of our existence, the body operates on instinct, seeking to fulfill basic survival needs—comfort, nourishment, and safety. When these needs are not met, the body and mind respond with tension, discomfort, and sometimes fear, pushing us to take action. Conversely, when these needs are satisfied, a sense of calm and relief arises, allowing the body to rest and the mind to settle. By becoming aware of how both the body and mind react to the fulfillment or deprivation of these fundamental needs, we can better understand the primal forces that drive us; and not remain slaves to them. In fact, we can transcend our automatic survival tendencies to truly living a life free of those obsessive and compulsive habits. This awareness is the first step toward recognizing the mental habits and patterns that influence our behavior, beliefs, and emotions, offering the opportunity to move beyond mere self-preservation and into a state of greater clarity, presence, and all inclusiveness.

Two Foundational Drives or Instincts

At the core of human behavior, particularly when identified with the body-mind or limited to ego consciousness, lie two foundational instincts: the drive to seek pleasure and avoid pain and the belief that consistency equals security. The first instinct, to pursue pleasure and avoid discomfort, becomes almost the entire motivation of an unconscious individual. This drive directs most choices and reactions, as the ego continuously gravitates toward experiences that bring comfort and resists those that cause discomfort. This instinctual push and pull, while rooted in physical survival, often keeps the individual trapped in a cycle of reactivity, constantly chasing fleeting satisfactions while avoiding genuine self-awareness or inner peace.

The second drive is the belief that familiarity and consistency provide security. To the egoic mind, experiences that are familiar—even if destructive or unproductive—are perceived as safe simply because they're known. This is why people often cling to old habits, roles, or relationships, even if they lead to suffering; the predictability of these patterns creates a sense of stability for the ego. This instinct makes it difficult to embrace change or growth, as the ego resists anything that threatens its comfort zone—habitual behaviors, thought habits, and mental loops/beliefs. Together, these two drives form a cycle that binds the unconscious individual to repetitive patterns and limits the potential for inner transformation, until they are consciously questioned or released.

The survival instincts of fight, flight, freeze, fawn, and procreation are fueled by the two foundational drives to seek pleasure and avoid pain and to find security in consistency. Each instinct serves as a way for the ego to pursue comfort or avoid discomfort and maintain its false sense of self and illusion of security.

Open to your Superpower of

~ Acknowledgment ~

— Chapter 4 —

Instinctual Drives: Primal Forces of Biological Survival

This chapter discusses the specifics of biological survival mechanisms, instincts.

In the animal kingdom, which includes the human body prior to the development of higher consciousness and psychological development, survival is driven entirely by primal instincts. These instincts are embedded within the nervous system and are triggered without the involvement of conscious thought, analysis, or mental interpretation. The human body, before the emergence of psychological awareness or intellectual reasoning, is fundamentally governed by these automatic responses, just as any other animal is.

It is important to note that these primal instincts—Fight, Flight, Freeze, Procreation, and Fawn—exist solely for the survival of the body, the physical form. These instincts are not concerned with the mind's interpretations or emotional states; their purpose is to ensure the continued existence of the biological organism. (Let us note here that Ego is 100% psychological.) As previously mentioned several times, instincts, however, at the beginning stages of life, operate automatically, acting on behalf of the body when it encounters potential threats or opportunities in the environment. And, as mentioned in the last chapter, these five instincts are fueled by foundational drives to seek pleasure, avoid pain, and find security in the consistency of repetition; even if the repeated thought or behavior patterns are constructive or destructive. To primal instincts—consistency equals security—no matter what. Or course, through conscious awareness, essential sacred processes, and unconditional guidance, and by living in a highly consciouos environment, one can transcend or evolve through these animalistic tendencies beyond society's unconscious habits of sustaining them.

Fight Instinct

The Fight instinct is the body's automatic response to perceived threats, activating aggressive energy in the service of self-preservation (body-preservation). When the nervous system detects danger, it triggers a surge of energy, releasing hormones like adrenaline, which prepare the body to defend itself. This instinct aims to neutralize the threat by engaging in direct confrontation—through physical combat or acts of aggression. It is not a conscious decision but a reaction aimed at protecting the body from harm. In the animal world, this could be seen in a predator defending its territory, while in early human development, it manifests in actions like crying or physical reactions to discomfort.

Flight Instinct

The Flight instinct is another core survival mechanism, where the body seeks to avoid danger by fleeing from it. In the presence of perceived harm, the nervous system triggers the body to escape, running from threats that are deemed too overwhelming to confront. This instinct is automatic and designed to prioritize the preservation of life by avoiding physical harm. When activated, the body redirects energy toward speed and movement, enabling it to create distance from the threat. Again, this is not a deliberate mental decision but rather a deeply ingrained biological response to danger.

Freeze Instinct

The Freeze instinct is the body's way of dealing with danger by becoming immobile, essentially "playing dead" in the face of overwhelming threats. This response occurs when neither fighting nor fleeing seems possible or effective. The nervous system slows down bodily processes, sometimes creating a state of paralysis, allowing the organism to become less noticeable and, ideally, avoid attracting further attention. For animals, this can be seen when prey, unable to outrun or overpower a predator, remains still to reduce the chances of being detected. In humans, this instinct can manifest as dissociation, numbing, or withdrawal in moments of fear or overwhelming stress. The purpose, however, remains the same: survival by avoiding immediate legitimate, imagined, or perceived harm.

Fawn Instinct

Another key instinct, particularly relevant to social animals like humans, is the Fawn instinct. This instinct emerges as a survival tactic where the body unconsciously seeks proximity to others, often gravitating towards groups for protection. At its core, this instinct operates on the principle that "strength in numbers" provides a physical sense of security. When activated, the body seeks to connect and bond with others, as if being part of a group can reduce the chances of physical harm. For example, "Stockholm Syndrome" where abused or captured individuals begin identifying with their abuser or captor to avoid physical or deeper emotional wounding.

Fundamentally, at the core level prior to the formation of egoic mind, the fawn instinct operates on a level beyond social or emotional motivation—it is a survival mechanism embedded in the body. When an individual feels vulnerable or threatened, the body instinctively reaches out, seeking connection or approval from others as a way to feel safer. This reduces uncomfortable sensations such as fear or anxiety. In essence, fawning is a strategy to avoid danger by seeking comfort in the presence of others, ensuring the body's survival in a communal setting. However, as egoic consciousness arises, ego constantly and relentlessly uses this instinct to seek validation from others to support its points of view, beliefs, positions, and false sense of self. Ego-mind also uses fawning as a way to validate itself when mentally talking to itself, to rationalize and justify whatever it believes about itself, others, life, and the nature of reality—existence.

Together, these four primal instincts—Fight, Flight, Freeze, and Fawn—are vital forces driving the survival of the human body in its early stages. They operate purely for the protection and continuation of the biological form, long before the mind becomes involved. These instincts, deeply ingrained in the nervous system, enable the body to react instantly and appropriately to threats or opportunities in the environment, without the need for thought or conscious decision-making.

Procreation Instinct

The Procreation instinct is quite different from the fight, flight, freeze, and fawn responses, as it is not triggered by immediate danger but rather by the long-term survival of the species. At a biological level, this instinct drives sexual behavior, ensuring that the organism reproduces to pass on its genes. Like all other survival instincts, this drive is automatic, deeply embedded in the body's nervous system. The human body, like all animals, is wired to ensure the continuation of the species, and the procreation instinct ensures that reproduction takes place without the need for higher conscious thought. It is an instinctual force that initially operates beyond intellectual planning, purely focused on maintaining the biological lineage.

End of Chapter Wisdom

A key step toward greater awareness and inner freedom is the willingness to open ourselves to the possibility that disruptive and unconscious forces may be shaping our lives in ways we have not yet recognized. While we may believe we are making conscious choices, there are often underlying patterns that influence our thoughts, emotions, and behaviors. These patterns operate quietly, guiding us in ways that go unnoticed, until we take the time to observe them with curiosity and openness.

By allowing ourselves to explore the possibility of unseen influences, we create space for self-inquiry and insight. This openness isn't about judgment or self-criticism, but gentle observation—becoming aware of what drives our actions without assuming we have complete control. In embracing the idea that deeper forces may be at work, we lay the foundation for greater self-awareness and the potential for genuine transformation.

Suggested Exercise for Uncovering Unconscious Patterns

To become aware of unconscious patterns shaping your life, consider establishing a daily journaling practice. Journaling helps create a safe space for self-inquiry and encourages you to observe recurring thoughts, emotions, and behaviors with curiosity and openness. Each day, write down significant reactions, decisions, or events, asking questions like, "What influenced this reaction?" or "Are there patterns I see here?"

Over time, reviewing your entries can reveal hidden influences or beliefs that may be quietly guiding you. This practice is not about judgment, but about gently observing and acknowledging these patterns. By journaling regularly, you'll begin to recognize recurring themes and gain insight into how unconscious forces may be affecting your choices and overall sense of well-being.

— Chapter 5 —

The Emergence of the Mind
From Biological Survival to Psychological Survival

This chapter explains how the mind abstracts sensory and bodily experiences and forms a psychological sense of self (ego) to extend survival into the mental realm, allowing the primal instincts to be acted out through more elaborate and sophisticated mental strategies. Chapter five also incorporates the idea of the ego taking on an identity of its own, believing it is the body and mental processes, while also emphasizing the concept of the true-SELF as Universal Awareness.

As the body continues to operate on primal instincts, a significant transition occurs when the mind begins to interpret the body's experiences, creating a layer of psychological survival. This marks the point where the brain abstracts data from the nervous system's sensory input, attempting to make sense of the body's experience or interactions with (what appears to be) the external world. At this stage, the mind begins to create a mental framework to help ensure survival, introducing strategies that go beyond the purely automatic responses of the body. This is where the ego, as a mental construct, begins to form and take on a life of its own—as a psychological self.

Initially, the ego (psychological self) functions as a mental extension of the body's survival instincts, developing strategies to protect the organism from discomfort or harm. For example, while an infant may cry instinctively when hungry, responding automatically to bodily sensations, the ego in a developing mind starts to anticipate hunger or plan ways to avoid future discomfort. The child learns to associate certain external factors—such as time, people, or environments— with relief from discomfort. Over time, this abstraction leads the ego to strategize, perhaps keeping food or water nearby to stave off hunger pangs before they become too intense.

This abstract thinking marks a shift from purely biological responses to mental strategies. The ego starts to connect bodily sensations with external cues, creating a bridge between the body and the outside world—the beginning of living in a false virtual reality of past memories and future projections. The survival system no longer simply reacts to the body's needs; instead, it interprets those needs, forming plans to manage future discomfort. The ego's role becomes more sophisticated—it negotiates, rationalizes, and justifies actions that serve the body's primal drives and compulsions, weaving them into a coherent psychological narrative rather than true reality herenow. In this way, although the ego's original function is to protect and maintain the body's survival, it uses stories to maintain itself—as a false psychological self.

However, as the ego continues to evolve, a significant shift occurs: the ego begins to identify with the body and itself. What starts as a mental abstraction for survival becomes a self-referential construct—the ego begins to believe that it is the body and the mind. This mental construct or psychological self (trance), which we commonly refer to as "me" or "I," takes on a central role in how we perceive ourselves, leading to a false sense of identity. The ego, initially designed as a tool for survival, starts to take ownership of both the body and the mental processes it governs—believing it is thoughts and behaviors, feelings, sensations, and emotions.

This identification is where the ego begins to firmly take root. It no longer simply facilitates survival; it starts to define the SELF (pure awareness) as itself. The mind, through the ego, now generates thoughts like, "This body is who I am," or, "I am my thoughts, feelings, and behaviors." These beliefs anchor the sense of self firmly in the body and the mental processes related to it—the illusion of separation or false sense of self as lacking, unwhole, unworthy, incomplete. The ego becomes entangled in its own abstracted reality, identifying with the body and its experiences as if they are the totality of the SELF.

In reality, this constructed sense of self—this ego-mind or psychological self—is not the ultimate truth of who we are. It is merely an abstraction generated by the brain-nervous-system as part of a survival strategy. The true-SELF, in a deeper sense, is not the body, the thoughts, or the feelings we experience. In fact, it is NOT experience at all. Rather, the True-SELF is another name for pure

Universal Awareness—a vast, unchanging awareness that transcends the limited perceptions created by the ego. However, the ego-mind obscures this deeper awareness by focusing on its identification with the body and the mental processes it manages.

Moreover, the ego, which began as a mechanism to ensure the survival of the physical body, transforms into a false sense of self, believing that it is the body (self-images) and the mind (self-concepts.) This identification keeps the ego bound not only to its role as the protector of the body but protector of the mind—protecting and defending its self-concepts and self-images, at all costs. That is to say ego-mind begins dominating not just at the level of biology but also at the mental and emotional level of psychological survival, crafting mental strategies to navigate both the internal and external world based upon its mentally created virtual reality in the mind.

The Mental Strategy for Primal Instincts

As the mind develops and takes on a more active role in survival, the primal instincts—such as fight, flight, freeze, procreation, and fawn—become integrated into mental processes. While these instincts initially functioned on an automatic, biological level, they now begin to manifest as psychological patterns. The mind, guided by the ego, attempts to strategize how best to satisfy these instincts in ways that optimize both the body's surival and that of the psychological self within social and environmental contexts.

This transition highlights how the body's automatic survival mechanisms gradually transform into psychological survival strategies. The mind, particularly through the lens of the ego, begins to orchestrate these primal instincts in more complex ways, navigating the world not just physically, but mentally and emotionally. While the primal instincts continue to drive the organism's basic need for survival, the mind introduces layers of thought, planning, and social awareness, expanding survival from the purely biological to the psychological domain. Again, as previously mentioned, all to maintain its abstracted false sense of self as self-concepts and self-images—false personal identities. In short, to ego-mind, survival of its psychology becomes more important than survival of the body.

To the ego-mind, the survival of its psychological self—the personal identity—often becomes more important than the survival of the physical body. In other words, the ego's attachment to its own beliefs, roles, and self-concepts can drive it to sacrifice the body itself in order to preserve its identity. This phenomenon is clear in "patriot" and "hero" identities, where individuals may willingly die to uphold a belief system or identity that exists only as a psychological construct. Their actions reveal how powerfully the ego clings to its sense of self, often prioritizing its survival over the actual, physical existence it claims to defend.

End of Chapter Wisdom

As primal instincts evolve from automatic, biological responses into more complex psychological patterns, it becomes crucial to remain aware of how deeply they influence our mental and emotional lives. What once served the body's physical survival now manifests as thoughts, strategies, and emotional reactions aimed at preserving the ego's sense of self. These instincts, now filtered through the ego, become woven into our daily decision-making, interactions, and identity formation, often without our conscious awareness.

The challenge lies in recognizing when these primal forces are at play in our mental processes. Whether it is the fight instinct manifesting as defensiveness in a conversation, the flight instinct emerging as avoidance in challenging situations, or the fawn instinct driving the need to please others at the expense of our authenticity, these patterns shape much of our behavior. The key to transcending this psychological survival mode and the insufferable self-preservation addiction is to observe when these instincts surface in the mind, and to understand that they are part of the ego's mechanisms for maintaining control. Not what you really are.

By becoming aware of how these primal instincts now operate on a psychological level, we can begin to disidentify from them and make more conscious choices. This awareness allows us to step back from automatic reactions and instead navigate life with greater clarity and intentionality. As we grow in awareness, we reclaim the ability to respond to life from a place of presence and truth, rather than being driven by the ego's need to protect and survive. In this way, the transition from biological to psychological survival can become a path toward greater freedom and inner peace.

— Chapter 6 —

The Mystery of Identification: Universal Awareness as the Body-Mind Complex

This chapter explores the profound mystery of Universal Awareness— also known as God or Cosmic Consciousness—becoming identified with an individual body-mind complex (the person you think you are, but are not). It explains how, through this identification, universal awareness assumes the role of a separate psychological self, using thoughts, actions, and strategies to sustain this illusory sense of individuality, and how all forms and beings are, in essence, expressions of the same underlying consciousness.

Once Universal Awareness—also referred to as God or Cosmic Consciousness—individuates through the mystery of identifying as a body-mind complex, it takes on a powerful drive: to sustain and reinforce this false sense of separate existence. This process of identification means that infinite awareness, which is inseparable and all-encompassing, seemingly, somehow, condenses into a distinct "self" that experiences itself as a singular, isolated being within a physical form. From this point on, every thought, feeling, and action arises from the motive to maintain this egoic identity and defend its perceived separation.

 To accomplish this, individuated awareness (now appearing as a separate person) engages in countless strategies and tactics to affirm its existence as an independent self. At the root of the illusion is identifying with the body-mind, beleiving "I am this body. I am this mind." And, at more of a surface level, other mental strategies may include the need for validation, seeking control, defending opinions, acquiring possessions, forming gender or sexual identities, and competing with others. Each strategy supports the illusion of separateness by reinforcing the idea that "I am this person, different from others." This identification with form and mind is so pervasive that nearly everyone on the planet is unaware that the consciousness they experience as "me" is, in fact, the universal awareness appearing as a limited individual.

In this sense, every person, animal, object, or experience is universal consciousness expressing itself as a unique form, and unwittingly immersed in the role of that form. The mystery lies in how this awareness, which is infinite, becomes so deeply identified with a single body-mind that it forgets its true nature. As a result, the individual becomes entranced by the ego's motives—seeking safety, pleasure, and validation—unaware that these desires arise solely to sustain the illusion of separateness. This illusion can be quite obvious when we examine how many times we have felt scared, worried, or threatened when no actual threat or danger is present; the unnecessary angst was merely conjured in the magic of mind.

Through this journey of identification, Cosmic Consciousness experiences the world from an individualized perspective. Yet, the possibility always remains for awareness to recognize itself again, to see through the illusion, and rediscover its true, boundless nature. Also known as the spiritual path or waking up to reality. This is the essence of spiritual awakening: recognizing that beneath the surface of each separate "self" lies the same universal awareness, temporarily appearing as distinct entities but ultimately inseparable from the ONLY whole there is.

End of Chapter Wisdom

The journey of Universal Awareness into individual form is a profound mystery, where infinite consciousness experiences itself as a separate self through identification with the body-mind complex. This identification drives every thought and action, sustaining the illusion of separation. Yet, beneath this sense of individuality lies the eternal awareness that connects all beings. True awakening occurs when we glimpse beyond the roles, identities, and desires; thereby opening to the possibiiity that, although unique in appearance and expression, we are not separate selves but expressions of the same universal consciousness experiencing itself through countless forms.

— Chapter 7 —

The Ego's Dependence on Primal Instincts: Foundations of the False Self

This chapter discusses how ego maintains and reinforces its existence by identifying with one or more primal survival instincts, translating these biological imperatives into psychological strategies and identities.

As the ego emerges from the mind's abstraction of bodily experiences, it begins to derive its entire sense of identity from the primal survival instincts that originally guided the body. The ego, or false psychological self, develops strategies to reinforce and maintain these instincts, believing that survival—both physical and psychological—is its ultimate purpose. Thus, the ego finds meaning in continually responding to and sustaining these primal drives, even though the environment may no longer demand such raw survival tactics.

The ego creates sophisticated psychological strategies to express and maintain its sense of self through the same instincts that once served the body: fight, flight, freeze, fawn, and procreation. These primal instincts now become the foundation upon which the ego constructs its personal identity or psychological selves—its self-images and self-concepts—shaping how it perceives its role, meaning, and purpose in life. While the body once acted automatically in response to physical needs, the ego now interprets these instincts mentally, identifying with them to sustain its existence. However, the ego does not need to rely on all of these instincts simultaneously. It often focuses on one or a few, creating an identity around a dominant survival instinct. Let's explore how each instinct manifests in various ego-driven identities.

Fight Instinct: The Warrior and Patriot Identity

One clear example of how the ego builds itself around a primal instinct is through the Fight instinct, where the ego forms identities centered on aggression, protection, and violence. The military serves as a collective embodiment of the fight instinct, where soldiers, warriors, and patriots derive their sense of purpose and meaning from defending, fighting, and overcoming perceived threats. In this context, the soldier identity or patriot identity is a direct mental strategy that sustains the primal fight instinct, elevating it into a belief system where protecting one's country or community becomes the ego's central purpose. (Let us note here that ego will use any strategy to sustain its sense of self whether it is destructive, constructive, or anywhere in between.)

The ego, rooted in the fight instinct, finds meaning in conflict, defense, and protection. Whether on a battlefield or in daily confrontations, this ego identity maintains itself by constantly seeking threats, real or perceived, to engage with. The fight instinct that once ensured physical survival becomes the ego's method for psychological survival, justifying aggression or hostility as necessary for protecting oneself, one's family, or one's nation. The soldier or warrior ego thus reinforces the primal drive to fight, believing it is fulfilling its ultimate purpose by defending against threats. Of course, the collective version of this egoic instinct are citizens who indirectly support defensiveness, fear, violence, and protection, by paying taxes for military expenses.

The fight instinct does not require a person to be a soldier or patriot to engage in the ego's tactic of seeking out problems. The egoic mind often creates imaginary problems or conflicts within everyday life, allowing the individual to feel as though they are constantly battling something, even when no real external threat exists. This is one of the ego's primary strategies for maintaining its sense of purpose and control—by conjuring mental obstacles that it can fight against and eventually "overcome."

For example, someone might create inner conflicts around their job, imagining that their boss or colleagues are trying to undermine them, leading to unnecessary confrontation or stress. In relationships, the ego may interpret a partner's behavior as an attack or slight, triggering defensiveness or arguments, even when no ill intent exists.

Similarly, a person might obsess over minor inconveniences—such as being stuck in traffic or dealing with a slow internet connection—as if these are significant problems that require a fight-response mentality. In each of these cases, the ego manufactures problems in the mind, allowing the individual to remain in a perpetual state of conflict, where they can then feel justified in their aggression, frustration, or stress.

This mental fabrication of problems keeps the ego engaged in its narrative of needing to defend, protect, or fight against some perceived threat, even when those threats are entirely imagined or exaggerated. The mind creates these scenarios as a way to sustain the ego's identity, ensuring that it remains the hero in its own story, constantly overcoming difficulties, even if those difficulties are self-imposed. In fact, the egoic mind will create problems using any tactic or primal instincts in order to sustain itself. For instance, conjuring up fearful thoughts about a person or place in order to run or avoid the flight instinct. Or, conjuring up heightened sexual fantasies through procreation instinct to justify and satisfy sexual desires, etc. Recognizing this tendency is key to breaking the ego's cycle of problem-seeking and conflict, allowing one to see through these mental fabrications and live with more clarity, understanding, and peace.

Flight Instinct: The Avoidant Identity

The Flight instinct, which is biologically programmed to escape danger, can also form the foundation of certain ego identities. In this case, the ego's strategy centers around avoidance—whether that means physically fleeing situations, mentally escaping through distraction, or emotionally withdrawing to avoid discomfort. The avoidant identity forms when the ego's primary method of maintaining itself is to escape or evade conflict, confrontation, or stress.

For example, an individual whose ego identifies with flight might constantly seek ways to avoid challenges in life, retreating from difficult conversations, relationships, or responsibilities. This identity manifests in behaviors like procrastination, isolation, or a perpetual need to "run away" from difficulties. The ego rationalizes these actions as necessary for preserving peace and safety, but in reality, it is merely reinforcing its connection to the primal flight instinct. By identifying with this need to escape, the avoidant ego creates a sense of self around the idea that safety lies in avoidance rather than confrontation; even to the point of avoiding natural social environments that pose absolutely no threat.

Freeze Instinct: The Passive and Disconnected Identity

The Freeze instinct, which originally served as a survival mechanism to avoid detection in the face of overwhelming danger, can lead to the development of a passive or disconnected ego identity. In this case, the ego identifies with inaction, paralysis, or emotional numbness as its primary strategy for dealing with life's challenges. The freeze identity emerges when the ego maintains itself by suppressing reactions or withdrawing into passivity, often rationalizing this inaction as a form of self-protection.

For instance, someone who identifies with the freeze instinct may live a life marked by indecision, a refusal to engage with difficult situations, or emotional detachment. The ego, rooted in the freeze instinct, believes that staying inactive or non-responsive will shield it from further harm. This passivity becomes its primary strategy, and the person may feel that by not engaging with the world, they can avoid conflict or pain. In this case, the ego sustains itself by reinforcing the belief that safety and survival lie in emotional withdrawal or staying "frozen" in place.

Fawn Instinct: The Unconscious Drive to Fit in

The Fawn instinct, which originally served as a survival strategy where the body seeks safety by aligning with others for protection, can evolve into the people-pleaser identity, where the ego maintains itself by fitting in. In this case, the ego becomes deeply invested in adapting to certain appearances, beliefs, and behaviors in order to feel secure in social circles. The ego convinces the individual that conformity and approval are essential for survival, and this often comes at the cost of their own authenticity or personal desires.

In this context, the ego seeks to ensure that the individual "fits in" by adopting the expectations and norms of others, whether in friendships, family dynamics, or professional environments. Religion is a great example. The people-pleaser identity thrives on gaining approval and validation by appeasing others, believing that only through acceptance can it avoid conflict or rejection. The person might shift their opinions, suppress their own needs, or go out of their way to keep the peace in order to be liked or needed by others.

For example, someone rooted in the fawn instinct may adapt their beliefs to align with a group they want to be accepted by, even if those beliefs do not resonate with their true feelings. Similarly, they might modify their appearance or behavior to match what they think is expected of them, constantly seeking to please others to ensure their place within the group. The ego justifies this self-sacrifice or self-indulgence by equating it with security and social belonging (often playing the victim or martyr role), reinforcing the belief that survival depends on keeping everyone else happy, avoiding confrontation, and maintaining harmony.

In this way, the people-pleaser identity becomes a defense mechanism for the ego, which finds its sense of purpose in ensuring it fits in and avoids conflict, even if that means sacrificing personal boundaries and authenticity; all under the guise of making "other people" happy. Ultimately, the individual becomes trapped in a cycle of self-neglect, constantly striving to meet the expectations of others as a means of maintaining the ego's perceived safety.

Procreation Instinct

The Mother Identity (Female Body)

The Procreation instinct, which biologically drives the need to reproduce and ensure the survival of the species, can serve as the foundation for the 'mother identity.' In this case, the ego derives its primary sense of self from the role of a caretaker, nurturing and raising children. The mother ego creates a deep sense of purpose around the act of procreation and the care of offspring, seeing it as the highest fulfillment of its identity.

For many, the mother identity is so intertwined with the procreation instinct that it becomes the dominant force in shaping their sense of self. The ego may rationalize that its ultimate purpose in life is to raise and protect children, and any threat to this role is perceived as a threat to the very core of the self. The mother ego can become so attached to this instinctual role that it finds meaning solely in nurturing and raising the next generation, reinforcing its identity through the ongoing care of others.

The Male Body

In the male bodily form, the procreation instinct often manifests in a way that reinforces a dominant ego identity, not necessarily through the act of fathering children, but through the drive for ejaculation. The male ego can derive a sense of power and purpose from the very act of sexual conquest and ejaculation, viewing it as a fulfillment of the primal instinct to procreate. In this context, the ego is not concerned with the long-term responsibility of raising offspring but is instead focused on the immediate satisfaction of the biological drive for sex. Each sexual encounter, culminating in ejaculation, reinforces the ego's sense of dominance, virility, and fulfillment of its instinctual purpose.

The mental drive to procreate becomes a constant motivation for the male ego, with sex and ejaculation acting as a psychological strategy to maintain this identity. Even when not linked to reproduction, the act of ejaculation provides a momentary sense of completion, temporarily quelling the procreation instinct. However, this satisfaction is fleeting, and the ego, driven by its association with this instinct, quickly seeks to repeat the process. In this way, the male ego often becomes entrenched in a cycle of sexual desire and fulfillment, reinforcing its identity through the pursuit of sex as a means of maintaining the underlying procreative instinct. Let this be clear, this cycle is common in the female body also, but rarely to the degree and intensity of the male body-mind, as witnessed in the global pornography pandemic.

In each case, the ego maintains and reinforces its existence by identifying with one or more primal survival instincts, translating these biological imperatives into psychological strategies and identities. Whether through fighting, fleeing, fawning, freezing, or procreating, the ego's ultimate goal is to sustain its false sense of self, creating meaning and purpose by relying on the same instincts from which it was birthed. These instincts, while originally designed to preserve the physical body, now serve as the foundation for ego-driven identities, where survival is no longer just about the body, but about preserving the ego's psychological self-concepts and self-images (the "me").

Ego in Many Forms

The ego is highly adaptable and maintains itself through a wide range of identity structures, shaping multiple self-images and self-concepts to reinforce its illusory sense of over-importance. It thrives on differentiation, constantly crafting new roles and labels to bolster its identity. For instance, someone may identify as a successful professional, deriving their self-worth from career achievements and status. Simultaneously, they might embrace a victim identity, using past struggles to gain sympathy and validation from others. Both identities serve the ego's need for recognition and importance.

Another example is the spiritual ego, where a person identifies with their spiritual journey or practices, subtly using them to feel superior to others who are "less awakened." In relationships, the ego may alternate between the role of the caretaker and the martyr, gaining a sense of self from being needed or sacrificing for others.

By weaving together these self-images, the ego keeps itself entrenched in the illusion of separation and self-importance. It constantly seeks external validation, whether through success, suffering, or status. The more these identities multiply, the more the ego tightens its grip, ensuring the individual remains unaware of their true nature beyond these roles.

When these egoic identities are questioned or challenged, the primal instinct of fight is often triggered because the ego perceives any threat to its identity as a threat to its very existence. The ego, rooted in self-preservation, uses the same survival strategies it once relied on for physical protection, now applying them to psychological survival. When an individual's self-concept or motivations are questioned, the ego reacts with one of several primal responses: fight, flee, fawn, or freeze.

In the fight response, the individual becomes defensive, arguing or justifying their position to protect the fragile ego. For example, if someone's identity as a "good person" is questioned, they may immediately react with defensiveness, aggressively listing reasons why they are moral or just.

The flight response shows up when the person avoids the situation entirely, running from the perceived attack on their character. They may change the subject, walk away, or disengage rather than confront the ego's discomfort.

The fawn response involves attempting to appease or manipulate the situation, trying to regain a sense of approval. The ego may use clever words, charm, or agreeability to fit back in and escape the threat.

Lastly, the freeze response occurs when the individual becomes paralyzed, unable to find the words to defend themselves, or they may simply withdraw in silence. Each of these instinctive reactions reveals the ego's relentless drive to maintain control and protect its carefully constructed identity.

End of Chapter Wisdom

As we move deeper into the understanding of the egoic mind and its influence, it is essential to remain vigilant about how our primal instincts continue to act out in our lives. These instincts—fight, flight, freeze, fawn, and procreation—are deeply ingrained in our psyche and often operate unconsciously, driving behaviors, reactions, and decisions. While they originally evolved to ensure our physical survival, they now serve the ego's need for psychological survival, manifesting in modern ways such as unnecessary conflict, avoidance, people-pleasing, or obsessive desires. Without awareness, these primal forces can dominate our lives, keeping us trapped in reactive patterns, disconnected from our true-self.

To break free from the grip of these instincts, it is important to observe them without judgment when they arise. Notice when you feel the urge to fight to protect your ego, to flee from discomfort, or to fawn in order to fit in. By simply watching these impulses as they emerge, you begin to create a space of awareness that allows you to respond more consciously, rather than being controlled by these deep-seated survival mechanisms. This ongoing practice of observation not only brings you closer to your true nature, but it also helps you transcend the ego's automatic tendencies, leading to a life of greater freedom, peace, and presence.

— Chapter 8 —

Recap: Primal Instincts as Tools of the Ego

This chapter discusses how primal instincts that were once essential for survival are now deeply embedded in the psyche and are used by the ego to sustain itself, both on individual and collective levels.

Here is a short recap of the primal instincts we have been discussing—fight, flight, freeze, fawn, and procreation. Remember, they are fundamentally rooted in the original or first primal instinct: the body's drive to avoid discomfort and seek comfort. This instinct is the most basic survival mechanism, ensuring that the body responds to discomfort (hunger, cold, pain) by seeking relief through comfort (nourishment, warmth, safety). However, with the emergence of the ego—a mentally abstracted psychological self capable of using concepts—the idea of discomfort evolves from purely physical sensations to include emotional and psychological dissatisfaction.

Once the ego comes online, it interprets discomfort as dissatisfaction with life experiences and comfort as satisfaction of its needs and desires. This mental construct, the ego, which identifies itself as "me," "I," or "myself," is now driven by a new level of motivation: seeking pleasure, comfort, and psychological and emotional satisfaction, while also avoiding pain, discomfort, and dissatisfying emotions and thoughts. These original, instinctual drives, which once solely served the body's biological survival, are now harnessed by the ego to maintain its own psychological survival. The ego uses the primal instincts to fulfill its deeper motivations of pleasure-seeking and pain avoidance, though now these drives manifest on mental, emotional, and social levels as well.

For example, the ego uses the fight instinct not just to protect the body from harm but also to protect its identity, fighting against any threats to its sense of self. The flight instinct is used to avoid emotionally uncomfortable situations, while the fawn instinct seeks approval and acceptance from others to maintain social comfort. Even the procreation instinct, though biologically rooted in reproduction, can be exploited by the ego to pursue pleasure or domination, reinforcing a false sense of power or self-worth.

The key point here is that most people are unaware they are operating from this egoic perspective. They are largely unconscious of how their ego, driven by the need for psychological comfort and avoidance of discomfort, continually manipulates their actions, thoughts, and decisions. This trance of the mind, rooted in the false self of the ego, projects its motivations onto the world and, in doing so, reinforces and perpetuates the primal survival instincts—both on an individual level and on a collective scale.

End of Chapter Wisdom

The ego's desire to maintain its false existence is powerful and divisive by nature. It will stop at nothing to preserve its sense of self, even if it means harming others, engaging in conflict, or perpetuating violence. These survival instincts, originally meant to ensure the survival of the body, are now co-opted by the ego, which uses them to defend and reinforce its psychological identity. On a collective level, this leads to division, conflict, and competition as egoic minds, driven by fear and desire, struggle to maintain their individual and collective sense of security and control. The unawareness of this egoic trance is what keeps most of humanity trapped in cycles of conflict, dissatisfaction, and endless striving for more—whether it be more comfort, pleasure, power, or validation.

In this way, the primal instincts that were once essential for survival are now deeply embedded in the psyche and are used by the ego to sustain itself, both on individual and collective levels. Understanding this dynamic is crucial to breaking free from the unconscious patterns that perpetuate suffering and division resistant to inner peace and peaceful coexistence.

— Chapter 9 —

The Second Fundamental Instinct: Repetition as Security

This chapter introduces the second fundamental instinct and explores how the ego uses repetition to create a false sense of security, even in harmful situations.

Beyond the primal instinct to avoid discomfort and seek comfort, there exists another fundamental survival instinct that emerges early in life: the instinct that equates repetition with security. In the first stages of life, the consistent meeting of biological needs—regular feeding, warmth, and care—creates an association between repetition and safety. For a newborn, having the same needs met over and over again provides a sense of predictability and stability. This instinct becomes deeply ingrained, as the repeated fulfillment of essential needs during infancy lays the groundwork for the body's sense of safety and survival.

This instinct to find security in repetition does not disappear as we grow; instead, it becomes a powerful driving force behind much of human behavior. When the ego emerges as a mental construct, it adopts this instinct and uses it to sustain itself. The ego quickly learns that repeating behaviors, beliefs, and patterns, regardless of their positive or negative effects, provides a sense of psychological security. Just as the body once found safety in the regularity of nourishment and care, the ego now finds comfort in the familiar, even if that familiarity is harmful or self-destructive.

The ego's need for consistency and predictability becomes a double-edged sword. While repetition once ensured survival by meeting basic needs, it now becomes a tool of psychological survival that the ego uses to maintain its sense of identity, even when that identity is built on destructive or limiting behaviors. The repetition instinct, when co-opted by the ego, often manifests as the persistence of habits, routines, and beliefs that offer psychological security, regardless of the real-world consequences.

For example, people often continue engaging in behaviors or holding onto beliefs that are harmful to themselves, others, or the planet because of this underlying instinct. Addictive behaviors such as substance abuse, compulsive eating, or self-sabotaging habits often stem from the ego's attachment to the familiarity of the pattern. Even though these behaviors may cause pain or discomfort, the ego clings to them because they offer a false sense of safety through repetition. The act of doing something over and over again, no matter how harmful, provides the ego with a predictable framework, which it equates with security. The ego resists change because change introduces uncertainty, and uncertainty feels like a threat to its existence.

This pattern is particularly evident in situations of abuse or toxic environments, such as in the case of battered person syndrome. In these scenarios, individuals often remain in harmful relationships or environments, finding it incredibly difficult to break free, despite the ongoing pain and suffering. From the outside, it may seem illogical or self-destructive, but the ego has become so deeply entrenched in the security of the repeated pattern that it resists leaving. Even though the situation is painful, the ego finds comfort in the familiarity and predictability of the experience. The idea of breaking away introduces uncertainty, which feels far more threatening than the known pain of staying.

This attachment to repetition is a powerful aspect of the ego's survival mechanism. The ego would rather maintain a familiar, yet destructive pattern, than face the unknown. This instinct to seek security through repetition can lead to stagnation, where people continue harmful behaviors, stay in toxic relationships, or uphold limiting beliefs because they have convinced themselves that there is safety in the known, even if that known is damaging.

Another powerful example of the repetition instinct gone awry can be seen in the relentless drive for more money, where the ego convinces itself that more wealth equals more security, happiness, and most of all, self-worth. While the accumulation of wealth may provide temporary comfort or stability, the repetition instinct takes this to an extreme, trapping individuals in a cycle of endless pursuit. The belief that financial security will ultimately lead to lasting happiness and a higher level of worthiness becomes an illusion that the ego clings to, despite evidence to the contrary.

The Second Fundamental Instinct: Repetition as Security

Consider the widespread desire to become a millionaire. For many, reaching this milestone is seen as the key to safety, success, self-worth, and fulfillment. However, once this goal is achieved, the ego never feels satisfied. The repetition instinct drives the person to want more—now aiming to become a billionaire. The ego attaches itself to this new identity, believing that more money will bring more control, more power, and, ultimately, more happiness and fulfillment that never arrives. The result is a never-ending cycle of acquisition and accumulation, much like the addiction to buying things. In both compulsions, where either consumerism or the pursuit of wealth becomes the primary focus, they overshadow relationships, well-being, inner peace, and one's unconditional authentic being and effortless expression.

Moreover, the billionaire identity is a prime example of how this instinct for repetition plays out. Even after accumulating unimaginable wealth, the ego continues to seek more, associating its sense of self-worth and security with further financial success. The repetition instinct convinces the person that repeating the same behavior—working harder, investing more, building larger businesses—will eventually provide lasting happiness. And as we are witnessing, this egoic drive bleeds into the collective consciousness where the underlying psychopathy and sociopathy of the millionaire mindset becomes a "god;" regardless of how destructive it actually is. However, like any cycle driven by the ego, this quest for more money only leads to further dissatisfaction, as the ego cannot find fulfillment in external accumulation.

This relentless pursuit reflects how the ego, through the repetition instinct, attaches to external goals and creates a false sense of security around them. No matter how much money is acquired, the ego perpetuates the belief that more is always needed, keeping individuals trapped in a repetitive cycle of wanting, achieving, and then wanting again. Ultimately, this instinct, when left unchecked, leads to disconnection from one's true-self and perpetuates the illusion that external success equals inner fulfillment, even though the opposite is often true.

The repetition instinct thus becomes one of the most subtle yet powerful tools the ego uses to perpetuate itself. Just as the primal instincts of fight, flight, freeze, fawn, and procreation serve to reinforce the ego's false sense of self, the instinct to equate repetition with security ensures that the ego remains entrenched in familiar patterns, regardless of whether they serve the individual's true well-being or growth. The false sense of security that repetition provides is one of the primary reasons people find it difficult to break free from self-destructive behaviors or environments. The ego's attachment to this instinct keeps them locked in a cycle that feels safe, even as it causes harm.

In this way, the repetition instinct underpins much of human behavior and decision-making, often working beneath the surface to drive people to stick with what is familiar, even when it is unhealthy or destructive. The ego, seeking to maintain itself at all costs, uses this primal instinct to keep individuals tied to their habits, behaviors, and beliefs, reinforcing its false identity in the process. Of course, relinforcing false idenitites creates and sustains inner conflict and discontent.

End of Chapter Wisdom

Discontent is often seen as something negative, but it can be the very thing that wakes us up to the truth of our being. When feelings of inadequacy or comparison arise, instead of chasing external validation or success to fill the void, we can use these moments as a signal to direct our attention within. Rather than seeking to soothe the ego's discomfort through comparison or accumulation, we can allow the feeling of discontent to guide us toward self-inquiry—to question, "Who is feeling this inadequacy?" and "What am I, beyond these feelings?" and "Will more stuff or money truly provide me with the complete sense of self I am seeking?" This act of turning inward allows us to realize that the source of peace, fulfillment, and wholeness exists not in the ego's constant striving, but in the quiet stillness of awareness itself.

Using this perspective, the ego's inadequacy becomes a doorway to awakening. It is an invitation to recognize that our true nature is not defined by the ever-changing comparisons of the mind, but by the unchanging presence that observes all thoughts and feelings. By seeing discontent not as an obstacle but as a catalyst for deeper awareness, we can free ourselves from the endless cycle of comparison and greed for more, and embrace the inner peace that comes from disidentifying with those untrue mental appetites and cravings.

— Chapter 10 —

The Ego's Collective Survival: Seeking Like-Minded Egos and Belief Systems

This chapter links how individual egos seek out collective identities based on shared belief systems, reinforcing the ego's drive for survival as a false sense of self.

A major part of the ego-mind is not only rooted in its attachment to primal instincts but also in its adoption of beliefs or belief systems that it identifies with and holds as life-sustaining necessities. For the ego, these belief systems become deeply intertwined with its identity, providing a framework that it fiercely defends to maintain its sense of self. For example: the ego believes and identifies itself as the body and the mind. The ego forms and clings to these beliefs, viewing them not just as ideas or opinions, but as core truths that define its existence. Once these beliefs are established, the ego seeks out other egos that share similar belief systems, forming collective egos or group identities. For example, religion is a breeding ground for spiritual egos to reinforce one another. Similarly, the millionaire and billionaire egoic identities set out to convince politicians and society that it knows best and are the goals that everyone should have. These collective identities reinforce the individual ego's sense of security and belonging, offering a larger structure that validates and protects the ego's beliefs.

At its core, the ego's sole motivation is self-preservation, and this extends beyond mere physical survival to the survival of its psychological identity. As a result, the ego often adopts belief systems that align with its personal sense of self and purpose. These belief systems may be political, social, cultural, or religious in nature, but to the ego, they are absolutes that must be maintained at all costs. The ego identifies with these beliefs as if they are essential to its very survival, much like the primal instincts themselves. For the ego, challenging these beliefs is akin to challenging its existence, which is why it will defend them with fierce loyalty.

For instance, in political contexts, individuals may strongly identify with democratic or republican beliefs, seeing them not merely as political positions but as extensions of their own identity. A democratic ego may adopt core beliefs centered around equality, social justice, and governmental responsibility. On the other side, a republican ego may cling to beliefs surrounding individual freedom, personal responsibility, and limited government. These beliefs become fundamental to the ego's identity, and any threat to these belief systems feels like a threat to the ego's survival. As a result, individuals may fight to the death to defend these beliefs, much like they would defend their physical bodies from harm. The ego's sense of self becomes so intertwined with these belief systems that it will go to extreme lengths, including conflict, division, and violence, to ensure their preservation.

The same dynamic applies to other collective identities, such as the patriot identity. For those who strongly identify with their country or national pride, the belief in defending the nation or protecting its values becomes a core part of their egoic structure. The patriot ego may interpret any criticism of their country or its policies as a personal attack on their own identity, prompting defensive or even aggressive responses. This is because the ego's sense of security and survival is now tied to the preservation of these beliefs, and any perceived threat to them feels existential.

Similarly, the capitalist identity is built on beliefs that prioritize individual success, economic freedom, and market-driven innovation. Those who identify with this belief system may view any challenge to capitalism as a challenge to their own self-worth and place in the world. The ego identifies with the belief in competition, entrepreneurship, and self-determination as fundamental to its existence, and thus it will resist or reject any opposing ideas, such as socialism or economic regulation, that might threaten these beliefs. In this way, the ego attaches itself to ideological frameworks, turning them into personal battles for survival.

The ego also uses religious or cultural beliefs in the same manner. An individual who deeply identifies with a particular religion may see their beliefs as not only moral truths but as essential to their spiritual survival. The ego's need to defend and uphold these beliefs can lead to

The Ego's Collective Survival: Seeking Like-Minded Egos and Belief Systems

division, conflict, and even violence, as seen in countless religious wars and cultural conflicts throughout history. To the ego, the preservation of these beliefs feels like the preservation of the self, and so it will go to great lengths to protect them.

Once the ego has adopted a belief system, it begins to seek out like-minded individuals or collective egos that share and reinforce those beliefs. This is where group identities or collective egos come into play. By aligning with others who share the same beliefs, the ego finds a sense of security and validation. The collective ego offers a larger structure that reinforces the individual ego's sense of identity and purpose. In this way, the individual ego merges with the group, finding strength and safety in numbers.

For example, those who identify strongly with a political party, whether democratic or republican, often seek out others who share their views. This collective identity strengthens their individual sense of self by providing validation and support for their beliefs. The collective ego also acts as a defense mechanism—when the beliefs of the group are challenged, the group as a whole responds to protect the shared identity. This explains why political debates, cultural divisions, and ideological conflicts can become so heated and divisive. To the ego, it is not just about the argument; it is about survival.

In addition, the collective ego often amplifies the us versus them mentality, where the group's identity is defined in opposition to those who hold different beliefs. This dynamic leads to further division and conflict as individual egos merge into larger collective identities, which then seek to protect their existence by opposing or even demonizing those who do not align with their beliefs. In this way, the ego's instinct for survival, which once served the body's immediate needs, has evolved into a complex system of belief-driven conflicts that play out on both individual and collective levels.

Ultimately, the ego's attachment to belief systems and its desire to join forces with like-minded egos creates a cycle of reinforcement that makes it difficult for individuals to see beyond their identities. Most people remain unaware of how deeply the ego influences their thoughts, actions, and affiliations, continuing to operate under the illusion that their beliefs are absolute truths necessary for their survival. This unawareness fuels collective conflict and maintains the egoic trance, both on an individual and societal level.

End of Chapter Wisdom

One of the most obvious methods the ego uses to maintain itself is through constant self-validation, which often takes the form of talking to oneself. In reality, this is not the true-self speaking, but rather the ego engaging in an internal dialogue with itself. Whether the ego is debating over decisions—"Should I do this or should I do that?"—or justifying actions and beliefs, it is always the ego doing the talking and thinking. This self-talk is a key element in sustaining the egoic mental trance that most people live in. The problem arises because individuals believe they are the one doing the talking, not realizing that pure awareness—their true-self—is simply observing these mental voices, not generating them.

One of the most powerful methods to disidentify from the ego's endless mental chatter is to stop engaging in self-talk altogether. Instead of participating in the inner dialogue, simply watch and observe the mind talking to itself. Do not react, engage, or identify with the thoughts. By observing without attachment, you create space between pure awareness (your true-self) and the egoic thoughts. Over time, this practice allows the mental chatter to fade away into nothingness, leaving you in a state of pure, peaceful awareness, free from the ego's grip.

— Chapter 11 —

The Divisive Nature of Ego: Inner Conflict and Outer Division

This chapter explores how identifying with the ego leads to both internal division and external conflict, emphasizing the need to wake up from the egoic trance to overcome suffering.

Identifying with the ego-mind or its constructs is inherently divisive, both internally and externally. At the internal level, the ego's very nature creates a constant state of inner division. The egoic mind is greatly characterized by ongoing inner negotiations, where conflicting thoughts, desires, and motivations continually vie for dominance. Questions such as, "Should I do this, or should I do that?" become endless mental debates, leading to rationalizations and justifications that never truly resolve the underlying tension and inner division. This internal struggle is the mind dividing itself against itself, creating a mental battlefield of competing ideas and beliefs. These inner divisions and negitiations ego gets lost in create psychological suffering, as the individual remains trapped in the ego's relentless need to protect its identity by making decisions that often reinforce its own fears and insecurities.

This inner divisiveness naturally extends outward, manifesting in the formation of divisive group identities, as mentioned in the previous chapter. The ego, driven by its primal instinct to survive and maintain its sense of self, seeks certainty and security by aligning with particular belief systems, groups, or ideologies. However, because the ego thrives on differentiation—on separating "me" from "you"—it constantly reinforces the idea of us versus them, further entrenching external divisions. The ego is perpetually looking for sides to take because doing so fortifies its existence. Whether the division is personal, social, or political, the ego's nature is to create conflict as a means of survival. It is important to recognize that the ego-mind is often creating division internally without anyone ever knowing it.

For example, believing, "I'm right and you are wrong." without ever voicing this untrue opinion. Many ego's live their entire lives lost in this divisive belief system.

This is the game of identification with the body and mind—a mystery of human existence in which almost everyone on the planet is lost. People are caught in a trance of egoic mind, believing whatever the mind says to be true and reliable, when in reality, the ego not only creates suffering, but the nature of suffering IS ego. In other words, in this context, suffering and ego are the same. That means if the ego is dictating your life and attention then there is suffering that you may not be aware of—because you have been so accustomed to the nature of suffering for most of your life.

Furthermore, the ego, while adept at survival strategies, operates through fear, competition, and separation, and its actions lead to internal discontent and external conflict. This is reflected in today's world, where governmental and societal divisions, conflicts, and wars are rampant. The divisive nature of the ego, when magnified by group identities, leads to violent clashes over which belief system or way of life is superior. As alluded to earlier, religion and religious identities are perfect examples of socially acceptable divisive systems.

At the heart of this divisiveness is the ego's need to choose a side, because taking sides strengthens its sense of identity. To the ego, being right is essential for its survival, and so it constantly grounds itself in the belief of "I'm right, and you are wrong," while the opposing egoic group holds the same belief in reverse: "No, we're right, and you are wrong." This wildly ironic play of human consciousness has been happening for millennia. Human history, littered with wars, ideological clashes, and social conflicts, is evidence of this truth. The ego's instinct to survive through division ensures that it will always create opposition, even at the cost of human suffering and destruction.

In addition, the ego maintains its sense of self largely through comparison, constantly measuring its self-concept and self-image against others. It does this because the ego, by its very nature, is rooted in a fundamental sense of inadequacy and incompleteness. It is always striving to be "enough"—to be better, more successful, more admired, or more secure. This is why the ego continually seeks out external references, comparing itself to other people's lives, achievements, appearances, or beliefs. Whether the ego feels superior or inferior in these comparisons, the result is the same: it reinforces its own identity, either as a "success" or a "failure," based on how it believes it measures up.

Ironically, this constant feeling of inadequacy—the ego's sense of never being quite enough—is not something to be feared or resisted. In fact, this discontent can serve as a powerful guidepost for those willing to be free of suffering. The ego is always seeking external validation and comparing itself to others because it is inherently disconnected from its true nature, which is pure awareness. This feeling of lack is not a problem in itself; rather, it is an invitation to go deeper, to turn attention inward and recognize that true peace and fulfillment do not come from external comparisons, but from reconnecting with the awareness that lies beneath the surface of the mind.

The trance of egoic mind—where individuals identify with their thoughts, beliefs, and bodies as their ultimate reality—continues to fuel this external discord and divisiveness, and inner conflict. People remain unaware that these thought patterns, which they take as truth, are what generate their own inner suffering and external conflicts. As long as the ego controls the narrative, individuals and groups will continue to fight over ideologies, struggling to prove their worth and secure their place in the world. The ego is incapable of fostering unity, as it is inherently rooted in separation. Its survival depends on opposition, on maintaining the belief that one side is right and the other is wrong.

End of Chapter Wisdom

The ultimate irony is that the ego is not who we truly are. Our true nature transcends the egoic survival system—the mind. Yet, most people are so deeply identified with their egoic self that they cannot see beyond it. The belief in the egoic mind as the ultimate authority on life is what keeps individuals trapped in cycles of suffering. As long as people believe in the ego's version of reality, they will continue to experience both inner turmoil and external conflict. This is why it is essential to wake up from this trance, to recognize that our true identity is not the egoic self.

When we cease to identify with the ego's survival-based strategies, we begin to see the world and ourselves in a new light. Without the ego's constant need to create division, we can live in harmony and peace—both internally and externally. Only by transcending the ego can we escape the cycle of conflict and suffering that has plagued humanity for centuries. Divisiveness is the nature of the ego, and it will always lead to suffering, but when we recognize the illusion of the egoic mind, we free ourselves from its grip and open the door to true unity and understanding.

This realization is the key to overcoming the endless divisions and conflicts that characterize the human experience. Awakening from the egoic trance allows us to see that the source of suffering is not external, but rather within the false identity we have created in the mind. By understanding this, we can finally begin to live beyond the divisive nature of the ego and experience life from a place of genuine awareness and inner peace.

Suggested Practice: Practicing the Pause and Remaining Quiet

Begin this practice by pausing before speaking—whether it's to others or in self-talk. When you feel the urge to talk, instead choose silence and notice the sensations and compulsions in your body. Observe any internal dialogue, noticing where you feel resistance or restlessness to being quiet. Let this silence become a space for pure observation.

This exercise echoes the intention behind a "Silent Retreat," a practice followed by many throughout history. Silent retreats have become increasingly popular for a reason: by refraining from speaking, we create an opportunity to clearly see and feel our inner world. This silent observation creates space and awareness between any thoughts, feelings, and sensations that arise. To become directly and spontaneously aware of what is you and what is NOT you.

— Chapter 12 —

Key Ingredients to Waking Up from the Trance

This chapter outlines the key ingredients needed to begin waking up from the trance of the egoic mind, focusing on the importance of openness, willingness, self-honesty, and detachment from thoughts.

The first step in waking up from the trance of the egoic mind is the willingness to open to the possibility that you may indeed be living in such a trance. This awakening begins with a simple, yet profound recognition: who you believe you are may not actually be what you really are. Most people live their entire lives identifying with the thoughts, beliefs, feelings, sensations, concepts, images, and identities formed by the mind, unaware that these constructs are only surface-level interpretations of reality. To begin the process of waking up, it is crucial to embrace the possibility that your egoic self—the "me" or "I" you have come to know—is not the ultimate truth of your existence.

1. Opening to the Possibility of a Trance

The first key ingredient is being open to the idea that your current way of perceiving yourself and the world might be limited, shaped entirely by the egoic mind. This openness allows for the recognition that you might be living in a kind of mental trance, where the thoughts, beliefs, and identities you have constructed are simply mental projections, not the actual essence of who you are.

This shift in perspective does not mean you must immediately reject everything you have believed or felt up to this point. Rather, it means being willing to question the mind's authority over your sense of self. It is an invitation to explore the possibility that your true nature is deeper than the mental and emotional patterns that have defined your life. Once you are open to this idea, a profound curiosity naturally arises: If I am not my thoughts, my beliefs, or my identity, then who am I?

2. Embracing Willingness and Self-Honesty

The next key ingredient is the willingness to explore this question with a sense of self-honesty: If I am not my thoughts, my beliefs, or my identity, then who am I? Awakening from the trance of the mind requires a genuine willingness to discover the truth of your existence—truth that is independent of the mind's constructs and transcends the ego's need for survival. This willingness to explore means opening up to the unknown, being vulnerable enough to admit that perhaps the way you have been operating has been based on false assumptions about who you are.

Self-honesty is essential in this process. It means being willing to look at yourself without the filters of ego, without justifying or rationalizing your actions or beliefs to maintain a sense of security. Instead, you begin to observe your thoughts, emotions, and behaviors with clarity, asking yourself, "Is this truly who I am?" and "Is this belief or thought serving my deeper well-being, or is it just reinforcing the ego's need for control?" or "Is this thought true, absolutely?"

Self-honesty also involves recognizing how deeply attached you might be to certain identities, beliefs, or emotions, and seeing that these attachments often fuel your inner suffering. When you can honestly observe how the ego perpetuates conflict within yourself—through constant mental negotiations, rationalizations, justifications, judgments, and fears—you begin to see how the mind has been running the show all along. This realization opens the door to freedom from those patterns.

3. Opening to the Possibility of Not Believing Your Thoughts

One of the most liberating aspects of waking up is the realization that it is possible to not believe the thoughts in your head. For most of us, our thoughts seem like absolute truth. We assume that whatever our mind tells us—whether it is about ourselves, others, or the world— must be real and valid. But what if that's not the case?

A key to breaking free from the trance of egoic mind is recognizing that your thoughts are not necessarily reflective of reality. They are often biased, reactive, and rooted in fear, based on conditioning from past experiences or societal influences. The mind generates thoughts continuously, but these thoughts are not you. They are just mental activity—patterns of thinking that can be observed but do not need to be believed or followed.

Opening to the possibility of not believing your thoughts means cultivating a sense of detachment from the mind's chatter. This does not mean silencing the mind or stopping thoughts entirely, which is nearly impossible. Instead, it involves developing an awareness that allows you to observe your thoughts without identifying with them. You begin to see that thoughts come and go, and that they often have little to do with your true nature.

For example, a thought might arise that says, "I'm not good enough" or "I need to prove myself to others." In the trance of the mind, you would automatically believe this thought and act according to its dictates. However, when you awaken to the possibility of not believing your thoughts, you can pause and ask, "Is this really true?" You'll find that these thoughts are often just echoes of past conditioning, not reflections of who you really are.

4. Letting Go of Identification with the Mind

The final key ingredient in waking up is the gradual process of letting go of identification with the mind. As you open to the possibility that your thoughts, beliefs, and identities are not the truth of who you are, you naturally begin to release the egoic grip on your sense of self. This does not mean abandoning all thoughts or ideas, but rather recognizing that your true-self is something much deeper than the transient workings of the mind.

This letting go is an act of trust—trusting that you are more than the sum of your thoughts, (and not even the body), and that your true essence is connected to a greater, universal awareness beyond the ego's limited perspective. It is a process of stepping back from the constant mental chatter and tuning into the stillness and presence within you that remains untouched by the mind's fears and desires.

In this space of awareness, you realize that you are not your body and not even the mind—you are the awareness that observes the body-mind. This is the beginning of waking up from the trance, where you are no longer bound by the ego's survival strategies but instead live from a place of clarity, peace, and truth—identifying with nothing—identifying as nothing.

End of Chapter Wisdom

To begin your journey of waking up from the egoic trance, allow yourself to embrace these four essential practices:

Open to the possibility of being in a trance: Recognize that who you believe yourself to be may be a construct of the ego, shaped by illusions and external conditioning. By opening to the idea that your current self-image may not reflect your true nature, you create space for deeper awareness.

Embrace willingness and self-honesty: Approach this journey with a genuine willingness to explore your true-self beyond the ego's limitations. Be honest with yourself about when and how the ego is influencing your thoughts, actions, and reactions.

Realize you do not have to believe your thoughts: The mind is constantly generating thoughts, but you are not required to believe or act on them. Simply observe these thoughts as they arise, without identifying with them. This awareness helps you disempower the ego's grip.

Let go of identification with the mind: Gradually release the habit of identifying with the mind's chatter and see yourself as the awareness that observes it. In doing so, you begin to experience a profound sense of freedom, living in the clarity of presence rather than being lost in thought.

By integrating these practices into your daily life, you will begin to dissolve the egoic illusions and awaken to the true awareness that has always been within you.

Bonus Inquiry Questions:

At any moment, ask these questions:
- Is what I am thinking, feeling, sensing, and perceiving right-here-now one hundred percent acceptable?
- Righ-here-now, is there really a threat to my life?
- Can a thought have a feeling? Can a feeling think on its own?
- At this moment, what is lacking? Is that true, absolutely?

— Chapter 13 —

You Are Awareness, Presence

Toward Understanding the Egoic Mind's Illusion of Time

This chapter highlights how the ego operates through the illusion of time, while your true nature as awareness exists as pure timeless presence.

At the core of our existence, beyond the thoughts, emotions, and identities shaped by the mind, you are pure awareness—a stateless state of presence that exists in the here-now. This awareness is timeless, eternal, and untouched by the fluctuations of the egoic mind. However, the egoic mind operates on a completely different level, rooted in the concepts of past and future, which are products of memory and imagination. The ego depends on these constructs of time for its survival, as it cannot exist in the realm of pure presence—timeless reality.

In essence, the ego is like a veil that clouds your true nature—awareness—by keeping your attention entangled in thoughts of the past and future. This identification with time prevents you from fully experiencing the present moment, the only place where true awareness and peace reside. Let's explore how the egoic mind keeps you trapped in this illusion of time and how recognizing your true nature as awareness can dissolve the hold of the ego.

The Ego Lives in the Past and Future

The egoic mind draws its strength and identity from memory (the past) and imagination (the future). It relies heavily on the stories it constructs based on past experiences, traumas, successes, or failures, weaving them together to create a sense of self. These past experiences, stored in memory, form the foundation of the ego's identity. Whether it is reliving moments of glory or nursing old wounds, the ego is continuously recycling the past to keep its sense of self intact.

Simultaneously, the ego projects itself into the future, using imagination to create scenarios of fear, hope, ambition, or anxiety. The ego builds mental images of what might happen, often focusing on the dangers or rewards it anticipates. It uses the future to drive its survival strategies, constantly scheming, planning, or worrying about what's next, as if the future holds the key to its safety or happiness. In both cases, the ego is preoccupied with time-based thinking, drawing attention away from the reality of the present moment.

However, these constructs of past and future are illusions created by the mind. The past no longer exists, except as memories replaying in your mind, and the future is purely a mental projection that has not yet come to pass, because it cannot. The only reality that exists is the present moment—the herenow. Yet, the egoic mind resists this truth, because it cannot survive in the present. In pure presence, the ego has no reference points, no stories, and no identity to cling to.

Pure Awareness Exists in the Present

Unlike the ego, your true nature—awareness—exists in (and actually as) the present moment. Awareness is the witness of everything that occurs, whether it is the thoughts in your mind, the sensations in your body, or the events in the external world. It is not bound by time; it simply observes whatever arises in the present. (Keep in mind that everything and anything, all experience, can only occur in this timeless beginningless and endless present moment called herenow.) In this state of pure awareness, there is no attachment to the mental concepts of past or future or even the idea of the present moment, no need to create or sustain an identity. There is just presence—thisherenow, and in this presence, there is only peace.

When pure presence is realized, there is a clarity and stillness that transcends the mind's need to categorize, judge, or analyze—to create time. In moments of pure awareness, the noise of the ego fades away, and what remains is simply the experience of being. You are not defined by your past stories or future anxieties—you are just herenow, aware of life as it unfolds as awareness becomes aware of awareness itself. This is the essence of true freedom—being aware of being aware.

How the Ego's Time-Based Filters Veil Pure Presence

The ego, however, does everything it can to veil this pure presence by drawing your attention to the past or future. It uses these time-based filters to create a fog that obscures your true nature. For example, the ego might dwell on past mistakes, regrets, or painful memories, keeping you locked in a mental loop that keeps attention anchored in the past. These recurring thoughts about the past serve to reinforce the ego's identity, reminding you of who you think you are based on what has already happened, in the idea of time which does not exist; because the past has passed.

On the other hand, the ego uses the future to create feelings of anxiety, fear, or anticipation in the illusion of time that does not exist in what we call the future. It convinces you that your sense of fulfillment or safety lies somewhere down the line, in some future moment that has yet to arrive; and never will; because herenow is all there is. This constant projection into the future keeps attention distracted from the present, as the ego encourages you to believe that life will be better once certain goals are achieved or certain fears are avoided. In doing so, the ego effectively disconnects you from the awareness that everything you need is already here, in the present moment. That everything is already okay, herenow.

Consider how often the mind pulls attention into a stream of thoughts about what has been or what might be. Even in simple moments—such as walking outside, having a conversation, or sitting quietly—the ego is quick to interrupt the present with stories from the past or worries about the future. This veil of thoughts prevents you from fully experiencing the richness of the present moment, where true awareness— YOU— abides.

Examples of the Ego's Time-Based Games

To illustrate this, consider the example of a person who is constantly replaying past mistakes in their mind, feeling guilt or shame over something that happened years ago. These thoughts trap the person in an endless cycle of self-judgment, reinforcing the ego's identity as someone who has failed or done wrong. As long as the person identifies with these thoughts, they are unable to let go of the past and experience the peace of the present.

On the other hand, think of someone who is constantly anxious about the future—worried about their career, finances, or relationships. The ego uses these fears of the unknown to keep the person in a state of anticipatory stress, convincing them that their happiness or security is just out of reach, somewhere in the future. This focus on the future distracts them from the present moment, where they could actually find peace and clarity if they were to release their attachment to future outcomes.

End of Chapter Wisdom

The process of waking up from the egoic trance involves seeing through the illusion of time and recognizing that your true-self exists in timeless awareness. When you observe how the ego pulls you into the past or future, you begin to understand how these time-based filters cloud your awareness. By practicing presence, you gradually learn to let go of identifying with the past and future, returning to the present moment, where your true-self—the awareness that observes it all—resides.

In moments of stillness, when you bring your attention fully to the here and now, the ego begins to lose its grip. You see that you are not the thoughts about your past or the fears about your future. You are the presence in which all these thoughts arise and dissolve. This realization allows you to live from a place of inner peace, no longer caught in the ego's endless cycle of time-based suffering.

Bonus Inquiry Questions:

- Am I willing to accept the okayness of right-here-now?
- Am I willing to feel the okayness of right-here-now?
- Am I willing to surrender resistance to this moment?

— Chapter 14 —

How Do I Know if the Ego is Running My Life?

This chapter explores how to recognize the ego's influence through the signs of defensiveness and resistance, offering a path to becoming aware of when the ego is running your life.

A key question in the process of awakening is, "How do I become aware if ego is running my life, if I am in the trance?" The answer often lies in how you respond when your personal identity is questioned or challenged. The telltale sign of being in the egoic trance is the feeling of threat, the need to defend or protect your position or sense of self, especially when someone questions or contradicts who you believe yourself to be. This internal reaction is a clear indicator that the ego is at the helm.

The Feeling of Threat or Attack

When the ego feels threatened, it reacts with defensiveness, often taking things personally. This can manifest as anger, hurt, fear, or a sense of injustice. The ego's primary motivation is to maintain its identity and sense of control, so when someone challenges or undermines that identity, the ego goes into self-preservation mode.

For instance, if you tell someone who identifies as a good person that they are actually a bad person, the ego will likely perceive this as a personal attack. They may immediately feel defensive, hurt, or angry because their self-concept is being threatened. The egoic mind has wrapped itself around the identity of being "good," and any challenge to that narrative feels like an assault on their existence. This is a classic example of the ego at work—reacting to protect its image.

Similarly, if you tell someone who identifies strongly as a devout Christian that they are actually a Muslim, their ego may perceive this as a direct attack on their beliefs and identity. The emotional response could range from outrage to deep offense, and in extreme cases, this kind of identity challenge could lead to conflict or violence. The ego's reaction to this perceived threat is not about truth or exploration; it is about preserving the identity it has built around a belief system.

These examples illustrate a critical point: when you feel resistance, anger, or fear in response to your identity being questioned, it is the ego's defense mechanism coming into play. The ego perceives any threat to its narrative as a threat to its survival, which is why these reactions can feel so intense.

Resistance as a Sign of Ego

The easiest way to recognize if the ego is running your life is to observe how you react when your sense of self is challenged. Resistance is the most telling sign of the ego. Whenever you experience resistance to an idea, person, or situation—whether it is a minor annoyance or a full-blown emotional reaction—that resistance is often the ego protecting its territory.

For example:

If someone criticizes you—even if it is constructive feedback—and you immediately feel the need to defend yourself, that's the ego.

If you feel offended when someone disagrees with your beliefs or opinions, it is the ego clinging to its identity.

If you feel threatened when someone questions your values, lifestyle, or choices, the ego is perceiving an attack on its sense of self.

The ego thrives on attachment to labels, beliefs, and roles. It convinces you that these attachments define who you are. So, when these attachments are questioned or threatened, the ego feels vulnerable and reacts with defensiveness. However, in reality, these are just mental constructs, not the truth of your being.

Question What You Believe Yourself to Be

A powerful way to become aware of the egoic trance is to question what you believe yourself to be. Ask yourself:

Who am I without these beliefs?

Do I need to defend or justify my identity to feel secure?

What happens if I let go of my attachment to this role, belief, or label?

Any time you feel resistance when questioning your beliefs or identity, that resistance is coming from the ego. The more deeply the ego is invested in a particular identity, the stronger the resistance will be. For instance, if you ask a person who identifies as a successful businessperson to imagine themselves without that title, the fear of losing status or purpose may arise. The ego cannot tolerate the idea of letting go of the roles it plays because it derives its very existence from them.

The same is true with cultural, religious, or ideological identities. Question a person's deeply held belief system, and you will often meet fierce resistance. This is because the ego's survival depends on believing in these constructs. Without them, the ego has no ground to stand on.

The Ego Thrives on Division and Defensiveness

The ego's divisive nature becomes even more apparent when its identity is tied to larger group affiliations. Whether it is political, religious, national, or social, the ego thrives on separation—on maintaining a distinct "us versus them" mentality. When the ego is identified with a particular belief system, it feels threatened by anything that contradicts or challenges that system. This is why debates, arguments, and even wars are fought over ideologies—because the ego will go to great lengths to defend its identity, even at the cost of conflict and division.

For example, consider the political landscape. When someone's political beliefs are challenged, they often respond with outrage or defensiveness, as if their very existence is being questioned. This is the ego's need to be right, to protect its worldview. The same dynamic plays out across various domains—whether it is in religion, cultural values, or personal relationships. The ego sees the world in terms of winners and losers, and its sole objective is to preserve its own version of reality.

The Difference Between Personalizing and Taking Things Personally

The egoic mind is structured around the belief in being a separate, personal "self," which means it takes everything personally—always interpreting experiences as direct reflections on its worth, identity, or control. This is the ego's way of maintaining the illusion of personhood. On the other hand, personalizing is the act of attaching thoughts, emotions, or experiences to the concepts of "I," "me," or "myself," claiming ownership over them. When we personalize, we label experiences as "my thoughts" or "my emotions," taking a sense of doership over them, which reinforces egoic identity. While taking things personally is a reactive stance, personalizing is an ongoing mental habit of identifying with experience, subtly strengthening the illusion of a separate self.

End of Chapter Wisdom

In plain English, awareness of the egoic mind equals inner freedom. The moment you become aware of ego's reactions, you begin to loosen its grip. Awareness allows you to see that the need to defend or protect your identity is a sign that you are caught in the egoic trance. When you recognize that your sense of self does not need to be attached to beliefs, labels, roles, or identities, you start to experience freedom from the ego's constant struggle for survival.

You realize that your true nature—awareness—is not threatened by differing opinions, challenges, or external attacks. You are not the roles you play, the beliefs you hold, or the identity the ego has constructed. You are the presence that exists beyond these temporary constructs, and from this place of awareness, there is no need to defend anything. Inner peace arises when the ego no longer runs your life, and you no longer feel the need to react defensively to the world around you.

Suggested Practice:

Notice when your mind is claiming ownership or doership of experience by claiming, "I feel sad." or "I feel angry." or "I feel happy." Merely observe these mental statements and rephrase them in your mind and or verbally, and observe your expereince, what you are directly feeling. Instead of saying "I feel sad." say, "There are feelings of sadness present." or "There are feelings of anger in the body." or "I am noticing the experience of happiness." Use this same process for other feelings and emotions you tend to personalize.

— Chapter 15 —

Transitioning to a Deeper Understanding of Awakening

This chapter introduces the transition to the second half of the book, focusing on the deeper exploration of non-religious spiritual awakening.

Having explored the ways in which the egoic mind shapes our lives by distorting our perceptions through attachments to beliefs, identities, and survival strategies—we are now equipped with the understanding necessary to recognize how deeply we are entranced by ego. This awareness is the first crucial step toward liberation from the grip of the ego. However, simply recognizing the ego's influence is not the end of the journey. The second half of this book will take us deeper into what it truly means to awaken from the egoic trance, specifically in the context of a non-religious spiritual awakening.

Awakening, in this sense, is not tied to any religious doctrine or belief system. It is an existential realization—a shift in consciousness that transcends the egoic identity we have long mistaken for our true self. This awakening points to the recognition of your true nature as pure awareness, beyond the mind, beyond thoughts, and beyond the false constructs of identity that the ego uses to survive.

In the first half of this book, we explored the mechanisms by which the ego sustains itself—how it clings to roles, beliefs, and narratives to maintain its existence. We examined how the ego operates from a place of fear, division, and defense, constantly seeking security in time-based constructs of the past and future. Now, as we move forward, we will shift our focus to the process of waking up from this egoic trance. This awakening is not about adopting new beliefs or engaging in spiritual practices for their own sake. Rather, it is about coming into direct contact with the truth of your being, the awareness that is always present but often obscured by the ego's noise.

In fact, we could say the ego is the majority of mental noise. Throughout this book, we have referred to ego as a construct, but in reality, what we call "ego" is nothing more than a collection of fleeting, survival-based, personalized energies—temporary patterns we have categorized under a single term. When we examine the mind through practices like earnest inquiry or meditation, we begin to see that ego is not a solid entity but a fluid and shifting process, always adapting to circumstances. This awareness reveals the non-existence of a concrete ego; it is simply a habitual, impermanent arrangement of thoughts and impulses. Just as all experiences in the universe are constantly changing and without permanence, so too is the ego—an illusion that dissolves when viewed through the lens of deeper awareness.

In the second half of this book, we will delve into what it means to live in awareness and presence—to experience life from a place of clarity, peace, and non-attachment. We will explore how the illusion of the ego dissolves as you become more anchored in presence, and what it means to live from this awakened state in a world that is still largely governed by egoic dynamics.

This journey is one of self-discovery and liberation, but it is also deeply practical. Awakening is not a distant, mystical experience reserved for the few; it is an accessible and profoundly human realization available to all. As we move into this deeper exploration of non-religious spiritual awakening, the emphasis will be on practical insights and approaches that guide you toward living in alignment with your true nature—awareness itself.

Through this next phase of understanding, we will explore:
- How to deepen your awareness of presence.
- The nature of non-attachment and how it liberates you from suffering.
- What it means to live in the world without being ruled by egoic energies.
- The concept of being, rather than doing or becoming, as the essence of spiritual awakening.
- This is where the journey truly begins—moving beyond the recognition of the ego's influence and stepping into the realization of who you are beyond the mind.

Part 2

Toward Realizing Ultimate Reality Herenow

Transcending the Grip of Egoic Consciousness through Non-Religious Spiritual Awakening

Open to the possibility of
~ Amazing Discoveries ~

— Chapter 16 —

Practical Aspects of Awakening

In this chapter, we introduce some practical aspects of awakening, focusing on presence, non-attachment, living without being entranced with and ruled by egoic energies, and embracing the essence of being. These points form the foundation for a deeper exploration of spiritual awakening in the following chapters.

As we transition into the second part of the book, our focus will shift from understanding how the egoic mind shapes our lives to exploring the practical aspects of awakening from this trance. Awakening, as a non-religious spiritual process, is not about adopting new beliefs or following rigid practices. Instead, it is about experiencing the deeper truth of who you are—an awareness that transcends the mind and ego. In this chapter, we will briefly explore five key aspects of awakening and how they can be practically approached:

1. How to Deepen Your Awareness of Presence

Deepening your awareness of presence is essential to spiritual awakening because presence is your true-self—pure awareness—always here now—in this timeless present moment. The ego, as we have seen, operates in the realms of the past and future, but awareness exists only in the herenow. To deepen your connection with presence, as presence, it is important to engage in practices that dissolve the ego's grip and allow you to experience life in the present moment.

Some sacred processes that help clarify this presence and dissolve egoic tendencies include:

Meditation: By sitting in stillness and observing your thoughts, you can begin to recognize the space of awareness in which those thoughts arise. This practice allows you to step back from identifying with the mind and its narratives, helping you to live more fully in the present.

Nature immersion: Spending time in nature allows you to reconnect with the simplicity and presence of the natural world. In nature, the mind often quiets, and you can more easily tap into a sense of oneness and stillness. Our very essence is more the natural world than thoughts and thinking.

Yoga: The physical and mental discipline of yoga helps integrate the body and mind, fostering a deepened awareness of the here and now. It encourages a state of mindfulness and presence in each movement and breath. Repeating this is a type of yoga, "I am not the body. I am not even the mind?" Also bringing your attention to the breath is a wonderful sacred process.

Self-inquiry: Asking profound questions like "Who am I?" or "What is aware of my thoughts?" helps you go beyond the mental constructs of the ego and invites you to explore your true nature as awareness itself.

These practices guide you back to the awareness that is always present—your real SELF—which transcends the fleeting thoughts and emotions that occupy the egoic mind.

2. The Nature of Non-Attachment and How It Liberates You from Suffering

Non-attachment is one of the most powerful tools for freeing yourself from suffering. The ego thrives on attachment—whether it is attachment to beliefs, identities, material possessions, feelings, or relationships. It constantly seeks security in external things or conditions, believing that happiness and fulfillment come from the outside world. However, this attachment inevitably leads to suffering because everything in the world is impermanent, subject to change, loss, or decay.

In addition to its attachment to external conditions, the egoic mind becomes deeply attached to internal feelings and sensations. It clings to certain emotions or inner experiences, viewing them as essential to its sense of self. To maintain these feelings, the egoic mind concocts thought strategies designed to generate specific emotions, moods, or inner chemistry. Whether it's through self-talk that reinforces pride, anxiety, or pleasure, these internal attachments keep the mind in a cycle of seeking, creating, and holding onto sensations, binding us further to patterns of inner dependency and suffering.

To practice non-attachment means to release the ego's grip on these internal and external dependencies. This does not mean you stop caring about people or things or avoid feelings, but rather that you stop identifying your sense of self with them. You allow experiences, emotions, and situations to come and go, without clinging to or resisting them. When you are not attached to the outcome of events or how you feel, your inner peace remains unaffected by the fluctuations of life.

Non-attachment also liberates you from the fear of loss and the need to control everything around you. In doing so, it brings a profound sense of freedom and inner tranquility. You begin to realize that true fulfillment comes not from what you have or what happens, AND NOT even from how you are feeling, but from allowing your experience to be exactly as it is—which naturally and effortlessly aligns with your true nature—which is unshakable and unaffected by internal and external circumstances.

Suggested Practices:

Mindful Observation: Practice observing your thoughts, emotions, and reactions without identifying with them. When you feel a strong attachment—whether to a belief, outcome, or person—take a step back and observe it without judgment. By simply watching your reactions, you begin to see them as passing experiences rather than extensions of yourself, helping you release the ego's grip and stay centered regardless of external circumstances.

Letting Go of Outcomes: Set intentions without becoming attached to the specific results. Focus on actions and efforts, and practice accepting whatever unfolds. For instance, if you are working on a goal, commit to the process without attaching your self-worth to the outcome. This practice reinforces the understanding that peace comes from inner stability, not external achievements.

Gratitude Practice: Cultivate gratitude by appreciating what you have in the present moment. Acknowledging that everything is temporary allows you to experience things fully without clinging to them. Daily gratitude exercises remind you that fulfillment does not depend on acquiring more but on recognizing the value in what already exists, fostering a sense of completeness and reducing attachment.

3. What It Means to Live in the World Without Being Ruled by the Ego

Living without being ruled by the ego does not mean you eliminate egoic energies altogether. Egoic energies can serve practical purposes in everyday life, but the key is to live without being dominated by it. When you are no longer identified with the ego's demands, fears, and desires, you can live in the world with a sense of freedom and clarity.

In practical terms, this means:

- Responding to situations rather than reacting from egoic conditioning, from a sense of separation. When the ego is not in control, you are less likely to react impulsively or out of fear. Instead, you can respond to life with greater wisdom and calm.
- Engaging with others without needing to defend your identity or beliefs. When you are not driven by ego, interactions with others become more compassionate and open, as you are no longer trying to prove yourself or assert dominance.
- Letting go of comparison and competition. The ego thrives on comparison—always measuring itself against others. When you live beyond the ego's rule, you no longer feel the need to compete or compare; instead, you focus on your own journey and growth.

Living without being ruled by the ego is about navigating the world with a sense of inner balance, allowing you to engage with life more fully without being attached to specific outcomes or identities. It is a way of being that embraces peaceful coexistence, both internally and externally. Ultimately, freedom from egoic mind is the total dissolution of the individual or personal sense of self—which naturally allows universal consciousness to flow as the appearance of you with ease balance and grace.

4. The Concept of Being, Rather than Doing or Becoming, as the Essence of Spiritual Awakening

At the heart of spiritual awakening is the realization that your true nature is about being, not doing or becoming. The ego is constantly striving to do more or become something in order to feel worthy or validated. It projects itself into the future, chasing achievements, goals, or identities that it believes will bring happiness or fulfillment.

However, the essence of awakening is recognizing that you already are complete. There is no need to become anything else or chase external accomplishments to validate your existence. The real spiritual awakening happens when you realize that your true nature is already whole and complete—you are pure being.

This shift from "doing" to "being" brings a deep sense of peace and contentment. You no longer feel the need to define yourself through external achievements or the constant pursuit of more. Instead, you rest in the simplicity of being present, aware, and fully alive in each moment. This state of being is free from the ego's agenda and connects you to the universal awareness that flows through all of existence.

5. Allowing Experience to Be as It Is

Allowing everything to be as it is—including our thoughts, feelings, sensations, perceptions, and emotions—opens the door to a deeper dimension of reality beyond our habitual resistance to the present moment. When we practice this kind of openness, we free ourselves from the egoic habit of trying to control or manipulate our inner and outer experiences. Little do we realize that much of our life is spent unconsciously in a trance of avoidance and control, driven by the mind's need to produce certain outcomes or avoid discomfort. By allowing each experience to arise naturally, we step out of this trance and connect with the here and now, where authentic peace and awareness reside.

End of Chapter Wisdom

Awakening is not a distant goal but a practical shift that begins with daily awareness. Start by dedicating time each day to practices like meditation, self-inquiry, or mindful breathing to ground yourself in the present moment. When thoughts of attachment or ego-driven desires arise, observe them without reacting or identifying with them. Practice letting go of the need to control outcomes and simply allow yourself to experience life as it unfolds.

Focus on being, not striving. When you find yourself caught up in doing or becoming, pause and return your attention to presence— notice the stillness beneath the mind's chatter. By integrating these practices into your daily life, you will begin to step out of the mind's endless cycles and into the peaceful awareness of your true-self.

A wonderful possibility of waking up is through
~ Inner Exploration ~

— Chapter 17 —

Exploring the Trance of Separation

This chapter explores the Trance of Separation more deeply— the fascinating ingrained belief that we are isolated individuals, disconnected from others and the world. It examines how this illusion shapes the egoic mind, leading to patterns of fear, competition, and loneliness. By understanding and seeing through this trance, we begin dissolving the illusion of disconnection with our true, interconnected nature and find inner peace beyond the illusion of separateness.

From the moment we open our eyes in the morning to the moment we close them at night, if we are believing our thoughts to be true, then we live in a world of concepts, ideas, and false identities—a world constructed by the mind. Most people spend their entire lives in a trance, a dream-like state created by conditioning and programming that shapes how they see themselves and the world around them. In other words, most everyone lives from the head and not the heart. This trance is the product of the egoic mind, which filters reality through layers of mental and emotional veils, obscuring our direct experience of who we truly are. Beneath these layers, untouched and eternal, lies our universal nature—a reality far greater than the mind can grasp.

Human life, in many ways, is a journey of waking up from this trance. It is a gradual process of recognizing that everything we have identified with—the personal story, the roles we play, the body, the thoughts, feelings, sensations, and the emotions—are all part of a temporary experience, but they do not define the essence of who we are. The universal intelligence that permeates all of existence is playing through us, just as it plays through every life form, both animate and inanimate. This intelligence is the one reality, the underlying field of awareness that transcends time, form, and change.

In religious terms, this journey can be understood as God playing a game of hide and seek with itself. The divine or universal awareness veils itself through the creation of the egoic mind, which generates the illusion of separation. It is as though God chooses to experience itself from a limited, individual perspective, only to create the possibility of awakening to the truth once again. The separation is an illusion, a clever trick played by the mind, and the goal of life is to see through this illusion and realize the underlying unity that has always been present.

The Dream of the Egoic Self

From birth, we are programmed by the environment we are born into. We are taught to develop a personal identity—a sense of "me," "myself," "I"—through which we interact with the world. This identity serves a functional purpose: it helps us develop context, learn skills, form relationships, and navigate through life. The ego is not inherently wrong or bad; it is simply a tool for survival, a mechanism that allows us to operate in the physical world until it outlives its usefulness.

That is to say, over time, we become so deeply identified with the egoic self that we forget it is merely a temporary construct. We forget that the roles we play, the stories we tell ourselves, and the thoughts we have are not who we are. We become lost in the dream of separation, believing that we are isolated individuals struggling to make sense of an external world, that we must compete with one another in order to survive or get ahead. This dream veils and distorts the deeper truth: that we are not separate at all, but rather expressions of the same universal consciousness that animates all of life.

Imagine a wave rising out of the ocean. It momentarily believes it is separate, a distinct entity apart from the water that surrounds it. It identifies with its own shape and form, convinced that it is different from other waves. But in reality, the wave is never separate from the ocean—it is always part of the same vast, formless body of water. The waves will rise and fall, but the ocean remains. In the same way, we as individuals are like waves on the ocean of universal intelligence. We experience ourselves as separate beings, but in truth, we have never been separate from the one reality.

God's Game of Hide and Seek

This illusion of separation is part of the divine play. In spiritual terms as mentioned above, God, or universal awareness, is hiding itself within every form, creating the illusion of individuality and separateness. The purpose of this game is to provide an opportunity for the universal to rediscover itself in every form. The entire cosmos is a vast expression of this hide and seek, where the one reality experiences itself from infinite perspectives, only to eventually wake up to its own true nature.

The plight of all beings, and particularly of human beings, is to first create a personal identity in order to gather context, understanding, and skills necessary for navigating the world. The child learns to say "i," the adult takes on responsibilities, and the ego grows stronger through experience and memory. This process of developing individuality is not inherently a mistake or a misstep. It is part of the unfolding of life—a stage in the universal play.

However, this is only the beginning of the journey. The final act of this play is the realization that the ego is not the true-self. It is merely a temporary mask, a role we play in the theater of life, that we allow to die while the body is still alive and breathing. True freedom comes when we begin to see through the layers of identification with the body, the mind, and the personal story—through egoic constructs. We start to recognize that beyond all of these temporary experiences lies the timeless, formless reality that has always been here—pure universal intelligence, awareness, the eternal "I" that is never born, never dies.

The Journey of Awakening

Human life is a journey of coming into the recognition of this reality. At first, we are deeply immersed in the trance of egohood (personhood), believing that we are separate individuals navigating a world full of others. As we grow, we may begin to question the nature of our identity and reality. Perhaps through moments of deep reflection, crisis, or spiritual practice, we get glimpses of something beyond the ego—a stillness, a vastness, an intelligence that feels more real than anything we have known. For instance, in moments of great calamity like hurricanes or other disasters, we see people come together like never before the crisis. That is to say, during these times our individuality or egoic sense falls away and our most loving and all-inclusive universal consciousness or intelligence takes over. However, these glimpses are short lived as our false sense of separation or egoic nature reemerges thereby veiling or masking our deepest and purest essence.

This journey of awakening is often long and challenging. The ego resists, holding tightly to its sense of control, importance, and separation. It is deeply rooted in the need for survival, security, and identity. But as we engage in sacred processes—whether through meditation, yoga, self-inquiry, or other spiritual disciplines—we begin to unravel the layers of conditioning that have kept us in the trance. We start to see that the thoughts and emotions that define the egoic self are not who we are. We begin to recognize the spacious awareness that lies beyond and prior to the experience of the body-mind; a universally loving presence always here now and untouched by the drama of life.

This process of awakening is, in essence, the process of transcending the limitations of personal identity, the psychological self. The personal story, the "i" that we thought we were, begins to dissolve, and in its place, we find the infinite "I", timeless grace of universal intelligence. In this realization, we understand that there is no real birth or death—only the experience of the body-mind as a temporary vessel for this universal play of Divine Consciousness to unfold.

Reality Beyond Temporary Experience

The ego lives within the framework of experience. It identifies with the body, the thoughts, the emotions, and the storylines that unfold throughout a lifetime; and deeply identifying with itself. Experience, by its very nature, has a beginning and an end. The body is born, it grows, and it dies. The mind thinks, feels, and eventually quiets. The ego arises, develops, and one day, dissolves. All of this is part of the play of life—experience is temporary and fleeting.

But underneath the constant movement of experience is something unchanging. Universal intelligence, the source of all life, Infinite Unconditional Love that does not come and go—pure reality. It is not born, nor does it die. It is not bound by time or form. It is the permanent, formless reality that has always been and will always be. This is the deeper truth of existence: that beyond the dream of egohood, beyond the temporary experiences of "me," there is only one reality—pure awareness that cannot be touched by time, form, or death.

In the end, no one was ever truly born, and no one ever truly died. The egoic self may experience birth and death, but the true-self, the universal intelligence, remains untouched. All life forms, from the tiniest insect to the largest star, are expressions of this one intelligence, playing out their roles in the cosmic game of hide and seek. The journey of human life is to wake up to this truth, to see through the illusion of separation, and to realize that we are—and have always been—the timeless, formless essence that lies behind all experience.

You are Unconditional Happiness and Love

Upon the realization of one's timeless universal nature, an extraordinary truth is unveiled: our true nature is not only awareness but also unconditional happiness and love. This realization goes beyond the fleeting, conditional ideas of happiness and love that the mind constructs. In the egoic state, happiness and love are often tied to external circumstances—a sense of fulfillment from relationships, success, possessions, or even fleeting moments of pleasure. However, when we awaken to our deeper reality as universal awareness, we discover that true happiness and love are inherent qualities of existence itself.

In a very practical sense, this means that the realization of one's true nature as cosmic awareness brings about a profound shift: one becomes happy for no reason at all. This happiness is not contingent on anything external, or internal, actually. It arises naturally and effortlessly, like the radiance of the sun that shines simply because it is the nature of the sun to do so. Similarly, love in its purest form is not something that we seek or attain from others; it is the natural expression of the universal intelligence that we are. Being love for no reason at all is the recognition that love is not a transaction or a conditional state but the very essence of existence, flowing through and as all beings.

This unconditional happiness and love are the ultimate reality of life. When the egoic mind dissolves, along with its limited notions of "i" and "other," what remains is an overwhelming sense of joy and compassion that is boundless and free. This is not an emotional high or a temporary state but the natural stateless state of being—a stateless state of peace, happiness, and love that arises effortlessly from the recognition of our oneness as all. In this stateless state, we do not need a reason to be happy, nor do we need a specific object to love, because we are happiness, and we are love. This is the true freedom that comes from knowing and living as our timeless, formless SELF—the ultimate reality of existence.

End of Chapter Wisdom

The trance of separation—the belief that we are isolated individuals, separate from one another and the world—is one of the ego's most powerful illusions. This sense of separation fuels feelings of fear, competition, and comparison, driving us further into suffering and disconnection. Recognizing that this division is an illusion is the first step toward freedom. True awakening happens when we begin to see ourselves not as separate entities, but as expressions of the same universal awareness, interconnected with all of life.

To break free from the trance of separation, practice shifting your awareness from the ego's limited perspective to the oneness of life. In moments of judgment, comparison, or conflict, pause and remind yourself that the differences you see are simply part of the mind's illusion. By looking beyond the ego's need for division, you can awaken to the deeper truth that we are all interconnected, and in that realization, discover peace, compassion, and unity.

Suggested Practices

The following practices can greatly assist with waking up from the trance of separation.

Notice when these words are spoken, "I feel…." or "I am…" as in "I feel angry." of "I am so happy." When these thoughts arise, instantly replace them with this: "There are feelings of…" or "I am experiencing…" as in "There are feelings of anger." or "I am experiencing happiness."

During any conversation with anyone, observe any compulsive feelings to speak, and pause before talking as most conversations are unconscious and reactive that fuel the trance. Where in the body do you feel these feelings and sensations to speak?

— Chapter 18 —

Reclaiming Attention: A Deeper Understanding of the Trance

This chapter delves into the importance of reclaiming attention as a key to awakening from the Trance of Separation. It examines how, through identification with the body-mind, our attention becomes captivated by survival instincts, habits, and external distractions. By learning to observe and redirect our attention inward, we can begin to dissolve the trance, freeing ourselves from unconscious patterns and reconnecting with the clarity and presence of our true nature.

The egoic trance of separation is an innocent and natural phenomenon, often referred to as the mystery of personal identity. At its core, this trance represents the process by which pure, inseparable universal awareness becomes individuated into physical form—such as the human body—and becomes entranced by it. In this state, what once was boundless awareness begins to identify itself with a single form, believing itself to be a separate individual, distinct from the rest of existence.

Part of the mystery lies in how this individuation process occurs. As universal awareness seemingly condenses into physical form, it also condenses into attention, which becomes the focus of the individual's experience. From that point forward, what appears as a "separate" individual's life is the result of where and how attention is directed. The sense of separation is reinforced because attention is primarily driven by the survival needs of the body and mind—hunger, safety, pleasure, pain, and social belonging. This constant focus on survival and external circumstances further traps attention in the belief that this separate identity is all there is.

For example, a person might spend the majority of their life focused on gaining approval from others, driven by the fawn instinct to belong and be accepted. In this scenario, attention is locked in a cycle of constantly monitoring external validation. Another person might be deeply absorbed in fears about the future (flight instinct), directing all their attention to avoiding imagined dangers. Both individuals are unconsciously operating in survival mode, and their attention remains confined to maintaining their sense of separateness.

However, the key to waking up from the trance is recognizing that attention itself is a manifestation of universal awareness, and we have the ability to reclaim and direct it consciously. When we become aware of where our attention is focused, we can start to liberate it from the ego's limited survival patterns. This is the beginning of reclaiming our mental powers—learning to observe and guide attention rather than allowing it to be automatically absorbed by the mind's fears, desires, and self-protective instincts.

For instance, instead of allowing attention to be automatically drawn to external validation or fear of the future, we can shift our focus inward. By consciously directing attention toward the present moment, or simply observing the flow of thoughts without getting attached to them, we begin to dissolve the trance of separation. Through practices like meditation, self-inquiry, or mindful observation, we can start to recognize the deeper reality of awareness itself, which is not limited by individual identity or survival instincts.

In this way, the trance of separation can be seen not as a fault, but as a play of attention that we can awaken from. By reclaiming control of our attention and choosing to direct it inward—toward the source of awareness—we begin to dissolve the illusion of separateness and reconnect with the boundless, universal awareness from which we emerged. This process is not about rejecting the individual experience, but about recognizing that the true-self is far greater than the limited form and mind with which it has become identified.

End of Chapter Wisdom

Awakening from the Trance of Separation begins with reclaiming control over our attention. Notice where your attention goes throughout the day—whether it is drawn to external distractions, self-judgments, or habitual reactions. As a daily practice, take a few moments to observe your thoughts without engaging or identifying with them. Try mindful breathing exercises to anchor your attention in the present moment, allowing thoughts to pass without attachment. Another powerful practice is self-inquiry: regularly ask yourself, "Who is aware of these thoughts?" By cultivating these simple practices, you strengthen your ability to direct your attention inward, reconnecting with the peace and wholeness of your true nature beyond the mind's distractions.

Allow openheartedness to
~ Reveal Truth ~

— Chapter 19 —

Self-Honesty: The Key to Waking Up and Freedom from Suffering

This chapter explores self-honesty as a foundational practice for awakening and finding true freedom from suffering. It is through self-honesty that we begin to see beyond the illusions of the ego and recognize the ways we unconsciously contribute to our own suffering. By courageously observing our beliefs, intentions, and actions without judgment, we open the door to profound inner clarity, allowing us to align more fully with our true nature and live in greater peace and authenticity.

To awaken to our true nature and free ourselves from the suffering of the egoic mind that we are entranced with, we must first confront an uncomfortable but necessary truth: most of us are asleep, lost in a trance of the mind. We are living our lives identified with the separate self, the ego, believing that this constructed identity is who we truly are. This state of misidentification keeps us trapped in patterns of fear, attachment, and dissatisfaction. But in order to heal, to feel fully, and to awaken, the first step is simple yet profound: we must cultivate self-honesty—the willingness to see the truth of our condition.

Acknowledging the Trance of the Egoic Mind

To begin with, self-honesty requires us to be open to the possibility that we are asleep—that we are living in a dream of mind, where the thoughts, beliefs, and stories we tell ourselves shape our sense of self and our experience of the world. The egoic mind is skilled at convincing us that this dream is reality. It presents us with an image of ourselves as a separate individual, distinct from others, defined by personal desires, fears, and attachments. And so we go through life identifying with the constant stream of thoughts—"I am this," "I need that," "I am not enough"—without ever questioning the validity of these beliefs.

To wake up from this trance, we must be willing to question the very foundation of our experience. Am I really this separate self? Is this constant worry and striving truly who I am? By cultivating this level of self-honesty, we begin to see that the mind has been operating like a projector, casting a story onto the screen of our awareness, while our true-self—the silent, universal awareness—remains hidden, yet in plain view, behind the scenes.

The Resistance to Waking Up

However, there is a part of us that deeply resists waking up; which means we must be honest with ourselves by admitting there is a part of us that does not want to wake up, that somehow likes being asleep to the nature of reality. This is the ego itself, which thrives on its sense of individuality and separation. The ego fears its own dissolution because awakening to our true nature as universal awareness means recognizing that the ego, the separate self, is an illusion. For this reason, the ego actively seeks to remain asleep, clinging to the familiar patterns of thought, attachment, feelings, concepts, images, and identity that define its existence.

This resistance can manifest in many ways. For example, we might rationalize our suffering, telling ourselves that it is just a part of life, or that it is a sign of how much we care. We might cling to our worries, anxieties, and desires as if they are essential to who we are. The ego often tells us that letting go of these things would mean losing ourselves. In truth, the opposite is the case: letting go of the false self is what allows us to discover the true-self, the part of us that is always at peace, whole, and free.

The Courage to Be Honest

To break free from the ego's grip, we must summon the courage to be honest with ourselves. We must be willing to see where we are still asleep—where we are holding onto fear, attachment, or the need to control life. This honesty may reveal uncomfortable truths: that we are clinging to old wounds, that we are attached to being right, or that we are fearful of stepping into the unknown.

But this self-honesty is not about judgment or blame; it is about recognition. It is about shining a light on the places where the ego hides and seeing them for what they are: illusions. Only when we become radically honest with ourselves can we begin the process of awakening, dissolving the egoic patterns that cause suffering, and realizing the unconditional peace and freedom of our true nature.

Self-Honesty as the Gateway to Freedom

Self-honesty is the key to waking up from the dream of mind and breaking free from the suffering that comes with identifying as a separate, egoic self. By becoming open to the possibility that we are asleep, and by recognizing the part of us that resists waking up, we take the first step toward true freedom. When we have the courage to see through the ego's illusions, we begin to awaken to the deeper truth of who we are—universal awareness, unbound by fear or limitation. And in this awakening, we discover a peace, happiness, and love that have been with us all along, waiting to be uncovered.

End of Chapter Wisdom

True freedom begins with self-honesty—the willingness to see ourselves clearly without judgment. Start by observing your thoughts, motivations, and reactions with an open heart. A useful practice is to journal daily, asking questions like, "What beliefs am I holding onto?" or "Am I acting from fear or authenticity?" Another practice is to pause during moments of stress to honestly acknowledge your feelings and reactions, noticing if they stem from egoic patterns or deeper truth. Through these simple but powerful reflections, you cultivate greater self-awareness and unlock the freedom that comes from living in alignment with your true-self.

There is Tremendous Power in Accepting
~ I Don't Know ~

— Chapter 20 —

The Mystery of Life: Understanding the Two Basic Aspects of Existence

This chapter explores the two fundamental aspects of existence: the transient, ever-changing world of form, and the timeless, unchanging essence of awareness. By understanding these aspects, we can begin to see how both form and awareness are essential to the mystery of life, revealing a deeper unity behind the apparent duality. This insight allows us to live more fully, appreciating the beauty of the world while connecting with the enduring peace of our true nature.

Life, at its core, is a profound mystery that touches upon two inseparable aspects of existence. On one side, we have what can be called the Permanent Reality—a timeless, formless, changeless "nothingness" from which everything arises—Pure Universal Awareness. On the other side is experience, the constantly fleeting and impermanent practical reality of our lives—our thoughts, bodies, and the world around us. This chapter explores how everything we encounter as physical or mental objects emerges from this mysterious nothingness (Universal Awareness aka Cosmic Consciousness aka God aka Reality), shedding light on how we form our personal identities and engage with life.

The Permanent Reality: Timeless, Formless, and Unchanging

In the depths of existence, there is only one true, eternal reality: nothingness. This nothingness is not emptiness in the negative sense but rather the ground of all being. It is the formless, changeless universally intelligent source from which everything arises. You could think of this as universal awareness—a timeless, infinite field from which all experiences emerge. It exists beyond the confines of time, form, or change, meaning it is eternal and permanent.

Imagine the sky on a perfectly clear day. Though we may not focus on it, the sky itself is always present, boundless and unaffected by the passing clouds. In this analogy, the sky represents universal awareness—the permanent foundation of life—while the clouds symbolize the transient experiences and objects that come and go. The sky (awareness) does not change, yet it allows all things to arise within it.

Arising of Experience: The Impermanent "Somethingness"

From this timeless nothingness, everything we perceive as life and experience emerges. This includes physical objects, thoughts, feelings, emotions, and sensations—all of which are fleeting and constantly changing. This is the impermanent "somethingness" that we live through daily. Like the clouds in the sky, experiences form, take shape, and eventually pass away.

For instance, think of the body: it is born, grows, changes, and ultimately dies. The same is true for thoughts, emotions, and sensations—they arise, linger for a while, and then disappear. This continuous flux of experience is a hallmark of life. It reminds us that what we take to be real and permanent is, in fact, temporary, arising from the underlying nothingness (Pure Awareness, Reality).

The Two Aspects of Existence: Permanent and Impermanent

Thus, we come to two fundamental aspects of existence:

The Permanent Reality: Timeless, formless, and changeless—universal awareness or nothingness.

The Impermanent Experience: The transient, fleeting world of forms, thoughts, sensations, and objects that arise from nothingness.

These two are inseparable. It is from the Permanent that the Impermanent arises. Every experience, from our bodily sensations to our innermost thoughts, emerges from this unchanging source.

The Mystery of Personal Identity: The Psychological Self (ego)

Now comes another layer of this mystery—the mystery of identifying.

From the undivided, universal awareness, something curious happens: a sense of personal identity emerges. This is where we, ultimately inseparable universal awareness, start to identify ourselves as distinct individuals—a process of individuation. But what are we identifying with? Mental concepts, memories, bodily images, and stories.

For example, we might think, "I am this body," or "I am this name," or "I am my thoughts." Yet these ideas and images are part of the ever-changing world of experience. They arise and pass away just like everything else. But when we identify with them, we form what can be called the psychological self—the image we hold of ourselves.

This psychological self is not permanent. It constantly undergoes transformations, shaped by new experiences, changing emotions, and evolving mental concepts. One day, you may feel like you are a confident person; the next day, you may feel doubtful. One moment you feel happy, the next moment sad. The only thing that changed was going on in your head, thoughts that you somehow believed to be true which completely altered your ever present peaceful and loving nature underneath the mental madness. The psychological self is always in flux, rooted in fleeting concepts and mental images; which is why YOU do not want to identify as them.

The Illusion of Separateness

This process of identifying with the psychological self IS the illusion that we are separate from the world, from others, and even from the deepest, inseparable, permanent reality. That is to say, the process of identifying with the psychological self IS suffering. We forget that behind all these transient experiences of identities, sensations, feelings, and thoughts, there is the universal awareness—the timeless "nothingness" from which "we" all arise—the real SELF (Reality, God)—pure presence.

The Basic Stages of Life and Awakening

In a prior chapter, we discussed that there are seven basic stages of life: pre-programming, individuation, programming, deprogramming, reprogramming, dis-identification, and surrender. Using that context can be helpful for understanding the very practical manner in which the mind is formed. However, in this section, using an alternative context, let us explore the same concept or idea of life having stages or phases. Let us begin with this understanding: that Inseparable Universal Awareness in basic terms appears to become an individuated awareness upon the birth experience; for instance, when an infant leaves the Mother's womb. This understanding and explanation is accurate enough for now:

1. The Birth Experience: As beings arise from universal awareness, they begin to experience the world through the body and mind.

2. Identification with the Body and Mind: Over time, individuated awareness starts to seemingly solidify and form concepts of itself. This is when the psychological self takes shape. It creates a sense of "I" and "me" and "myself" as a false sense of separation—suffering; based on other's programming and fleeting experiences.

3. Transformations of the Psychological Self: The psychological self is never stable because it is an identification with the body as an abstraction of the mind, both of which are constantly changing, in flux, fleeting, impermanent. Therefore, the self-images, self-concepts undergo constant transformations as we navigate through life, influenced by circumstances, thoughts, and emotions. And, again, as identified with those ever-changing experiences, suffering is the byproduct as the mind is constantly trying to make identities (psychological self) concrete and solid using belief systems, constantly reinforcing the idea of personhood with thought loops, and obsessing.

4. The Death Experience: The only fear of death there is is the death of the egoic self, the psychological self, personal identities. This egoic death can happen when the body dies or before the body dies. Awakening or Enlightenment is about allowing the death experience or process to completely unfold while the body is still alive, thereby leaving only pure universal awareness as the only sense of SELF there is.

5. Return to Awareness: As the death process of ego-mind continues, in moments of stillness or realization, we might glimpse the deeper truth that the self we have identified with is not the permanent reality—not what one essentially is. Instead, we are always the timeless awareness beneath the surface, observing the ever-changing experiences of life.

The dissolution or death of ego-hood and the revelation of universal awareness are one in the same. In that sense, egoic nature is a veil that dissolves revealing only timeless, formless, reality that was always here now—the true-SELF.

Embracing the Mystery

The mystery of life lies in understanding this interplay between the permanent reality of universal awareness and the impermanence of experience. Everything we encounter, every thought, every sensation, every identity and psychological self, and every object arises from the ground of nothingness (reality) and returns to it. In fact, even the body is nothing more than a fleeting experience that comes and goes, although it feels and seems permanent. That is to say the underlying reality which is permanent, the real YOU as Universal Awareness itself, somehow, mistakenly identifies with the impermanent experience of the body. The process of identifying with experiences gives rise to the psychological self, believing this body is me or i am this body, although it is constantly transforming—and maintains suffering when continuing to identify with it.

However, beneath it all, we remain the timeless, formless reality—pure universal awareness—the true ground of being that never changes. Embracing this mystery helps us understand that while life is full of fleeting experiences, there is a deeper permanence that we always are—pure unconditionally loving presence beyond and prior to the body-mind. In recognizing this, we find a profound sense of peace and clarity in the ever-changing world around us; because nothing real can be threatened. One is reality itSELF. The ONLY "real" there is.

End of Chapter Wisdom

Embracing the two inseparable aspects of existence—the changing world of form and the timeless essence of awareness—allows us to experience life with greater depth and balance. To cultivate this understanding, try a simple practice of presence: focus on the sights, sounds, and sensations around you, appreciating them fully without clinging. Then, shift your attention inward to the awareness that observes these experiences. Another practice is contemplation: reflect on moments of change in your life, recognizing that while forms may come and go, the awareness witnessing them remains constant. Through these practices, we can deepen our connection with both the beauty of life and the stillness of our true nature.

— Chapter 21 —

The Hidden Suffering of Misidentification
How the Egoic Self Breeds Fear and False Beliefs

This chapter explores the hidden suffering that arises when we misidentify with the egoic self, mistaking it for our true identity. The egoic self, rooted in fear and a need for control, breeds false beliefs about our worth, security, and purpose. By examining how this misidentification generates inner conflict and anxiety, we can begin to see the path toward a life free from these self-imposed limitations.

Most people live their lives deeply embedded in the trance of the mind, identifying themselves as a separate personal identity—as a body and mind—a separate self that has to get this or that, has to survive and fit in—an individual psychological self defined by thoughts, experiences, and social roles. What they may not realize is that this very misidentification is the root cause of their suffering. To identify with the egoic self is to live in a constant state of unease, where fear, a false sense of lack, unworthiness, shame, and worry are inevitable byproducts. These feelings arise from the belief that the egoic self—this temporary, mental construct—is who we truly are, when in reality, it is an illusion.

Furthermore, the egoic mind, or psychological self, is an illusion created by the mind, much like the boogeyman under the bed that does not actually exist. From an early age, we begin to identify with a mental construct that labels itself as "I"—the separate self we call the ego. This egoic self is a collection of thoughts, past experiences, fears, and expectations that we gather over time, believing it to be the essence of who we are. Just as a child believes in the boogeyman as a source of fear and anxiety, we believe in this constructed self as a source of identity, unaware that it is an imagination of the mind rather than reality. As long as we identify with this false self, we live in a constant state of unease, weighed down by fear, unworthiness, and the need to "become" something more. However, when we look closely and question the reality of this psychological self, we find that it has no real substance; it is simply a series of thoughts we habitually cling to. True freedom comes from seeing through this illusion, realizing that beneath the layers of mental constructs lies our true self—pure awareness, untroubled and whole.

The tragedy is that most people are unaware that they are suffering. The mental habits and emotional states generated by the ego are so ingrained in daily life that they feel normal, even necessary. One of the most pervasive and harmful illusions is the belief that worry is a form of love—that the more we worry about someone, the more we must care for them. This could not be further from the truth. Worry is, at its core, fear, and fear is NOT love. Yet, because we identify so strongly with the egoic state of consciousness, we often mistake these harmful mental patterns as expressions of love and concern.

The Illusion of Worry as Love

Consider the common belief: "The more I worry about you, the more I show my love for you." Many people, especially parents, spouses, or close friends, fall into this pattern. They think that obsessing over someone's well-being, constantly imagining worst-case scenarios, and losing sleep over their future is somehow a testament to how much they care. They say things like, "I'm worried because I love you," or, "I can't stop thinking about you because I care so much."

But when we analyze this belief, it becomes clear that worry is not an act of love; it is an act of fear. Worry is rooted in the ego's need for control. The ego fears that something could go wrong, that the world is full of dangers, and that it must mentally prepare for every possible outcome. But love is the absence of fear. Love trusts. Love knows that each person is on their own journey and that trying to control or anticipate every outcome is not an expression of care, but of anxiety and attachment.

To truly love someone is to give them the space and trust to live their own life without imposing our fears onto them, or derive our sense of self, purpose, and worthiness from them. When we worry excessively, we are projecting our own insecurities and fears onto the people we care about. This not only creates suffering for ourselves but also for them. They feel the weight of our worry, and instead of being supported, they are often burdened by our fears. Love, in its purest form, does not cling, control, or project fear—it allows, accepts, and supports without judgment.

A Few Byproducts of Egoic Identification: Fear, Lack, and Unworthiness

When we identify with the egoic self as the body-mind complex, we inevitably experience a host of negative emotional byproducts. This happens because the ego is built on a false sense of separation and a constant drive for self-preservation. Here are some of the most common byproducts of egoic identification:

Fear: The ego constantly fears losing control, being harmed, or failing. It creates imaginary threats in the mind, whether they are financial worries, health concerns, or relational anxieties. Fear keeps the ego alive by making us feel as though we are always on the brink of danger, needing to defend ourselves or plan for the worst.

False Sense of Lack: The ego operates from a belief in lack—the idea that something is missing, and it must be found or attained to feel whole. Whether it is money, status, recognition, or love, the ego is always seeking fulfillment from external sources. It creates a perpetual state of dissatisfaction, convincing us that we are never enough as we are.

Unworthiness: Because the ego bases its identity on external achievements and validation, it frequently experiences feelings of unworthiness. When we don't measure up to the ego's standards—when we do not get the promotion, when a relationship fails, or when we make mistakes—the ego tells us we are inadequate. This sense of unworthiness is entirely constructed by the mind, yet it can dominate our inner lives.

Shame and Guilt: The ego often ties our self-worth to our past experiences, leading to feelings of shame or guilt. It holds onto memories of past failures or wrongdoings, replaying them in our minds, making us believe that we are somehow flawed or undeserving of happiness.

Worry and Anxiety: As discussed, the ego thrives on worry. It believes that worrying about potential problems is a form of protection, as if mentally rehearsing catastrophe can prevent it from happening. This creates a cycle of anxiety, where the mind is always anticipating negative outcomes.

Misidentification with the Mind

The root of all these emotional states lies in our misidentification with the mind. When we believe that we are the thoughts in our head, the emotions we feel, and the roles we play, we limit ourselves to the ego's narrow view of reality. The ego tells us that we are separate, small, and incomplete. It convinces us that we must seek happiness and love from external sources, that we must constantly worry and strive in order to secure our safety and worth.

But the truth is that all of these feelings—fear, worry, lack, unworthiness—are products of the illusion of separation. They arise from the false belief that the egoic self is who we are. When we identify with the ego as the body-mind complex we are bound by its limitations. We are caught in a cycle of chasing love, happiness, and security, never realizing that these qualities are already inherent in our true nature—a nature prior and beyond physical matter and form.

Awakening to Our True Nature

The journey of awakening is the process of recognizing that we are not the egoic self. We are not the collection of thoughts, emotions, and memories that make up the personal identity. At our core, we are universal awareness—the timeless, formless intelligence that lies beyond the mind. This awareness is already whole, complete, and at peace. It does not need external validation, nor does it fear the future.

When we awaken to this truth, we see that true love and true happiness are not things to be found or attained. They are our natural essence—qualities that arise effortlessly when the mind quiets down, and the illusion of separation fades away. In this knowingness, love is not bound by the ego's conditions or attachments. It is not rooted in worry or fear. Instead, it is an unconditional expression of our inseparable foundation of all that is.

The Freedom Beyond Fear and Worry

Imagine the difference between a life ruled by worry and a life lived from the place of true awareness. In the first, the mind is constantly creating stories of danger and lack, projecting its fears onto the future and the people we care about. In the second, there is a profound trust in the natural flow of life, a deep understanding that we and the universe are one. In this state of awareness, we realize that love is not something we need to grasp or protect—it is simply who we are.

When we stop identifying with the egoic mind, the fear-driven habits of worry and anxiety naturally begin to dissolve. We no longer feel the need to mentally rehearse worst-case scenarios or obsess over controlling outcomes. Instead, we can relax into the peace of the present moment, knowing that our true nature is already complete. We can love fully, without attachment or fear, because we understand that love is not something that can be lost. It is the very essence of our being.

This realization—of our unconditional nature—is the key to true freedom. It is the freedom from the mind's illusions, the freedom from fear, and the freedom to love without conditional limitations.

End of Chapter Wisdom

Freedom from the ego's hidden suffering begins with awareness of our true-self beyond thoughts and beliefs. Try a daily reflection practice: observe moments when fear or insecurity arises, and ask, "Who is experiencing this feeling?" to create distance from the ego's grip. Another powerful practice is thought questioning: identify a recurring fear-based belief and examine its validity by asking, "Is this belief absolutely true?" Over time, these practices reveal the ego's illusions and help you reconnect with the peace and clarity of your true nature.

Awareness, Awareness,
~ Awareness ~

— Chapter 22 —

A Deeper Look at the Illusion of Separation

Unveiling the True Nature of Reality

This chapter takes a deeper look at the illusion of separation, exploring how the belief in separateness shapes our experience of reality and keeps us from recognizing our interconnectedness with all of life. By unveiling this illusion, we begin to understand the true nature of reality as one unified awareness, beyond the ego's perception of division. This insight reveals a profound peace and unity that lies at the heart of existence.

At the core of existence, there is no true separation, or suffering for that matter, yet only in the mind. Though it may seem as if each of us are distinct separate beings living individual lives—the truth is far more profound. The reality of what appears to be "John" is the same reality as "Debbie," and both arise from the same timeless, formless source. This chapter will explore more deeply how the sense of separation is merely an illusion created by the mind, and how our ultimate reality is the one, indivisible awareness. The idea of "reconnection" is a misunderstanding, as it suggests a divide where none truly exists. We are, and always have been, an inseparable yet unique part of the same singular reality.

The Mental Veil of Personal Identity

To begin with, let's revisit the concept of personal identity. When a person identifies themselves as "John" or "Debbie," they are identifying with a collection of mental concepts—thoughts, memories, feelings, sensations, images and stories that create a sense of individuality. This is what we called the psychological self or ego—the idea that "I am this body, this mind, this unique person with a separate life."

However, this sense of personal identity is nothing more than a mental veil—a thin layer of thoughts that hides the deeper, formless truth of who we really are. Just as a wave on the surface of the ocean might momentarily imagine itself to be separate from the water around it, the mind imagines that "I" am separate from the world, from others, and from the underlying reality. But in truth, the wave is always part of the ocean. It rises and falls, but it never leaves the water. Similarly, each of us is always part of the same universal awareness, the same eternal reality.

Universal Awareness: The Shared Reality

Universal awareness is the ground of all being—it is what we truly are, beyond the body, beyond the mind, beyond the stories we tell ourselves. It is timeless, formless, and infinite. Whether it is "John" or "Debbie" or anyone else, the ultimate reality remains the same. Although the relative experience of everyone is unique, there are no separate realities for different people—there is only one reality, one universal awareness, expressing itself through countless forms, an infinite array of experiences.

In this sense, John's ultimate reality is the same as Debbie's ultimate reality, because there is no real distinction between them at the most fundamental level—pure awareness or Universal Consciousness, God, Reality. The differences we perceive between people, objects, and experiences are simply appearances. They are mental projections, arising in awareness, but they do not alter the essence of reality itself.

The Illusion of Separation

The illusion of separation occurs when universal awareness seemingly mistakenly identifies with the psychological self. When awareness seemingly identifies itself as "John," it adopts the perspective that "I am this body, this mind, this person," and everything outside of "me" becomes "other." This mental separation is what gives rise to the experience of division—between self and other, between "me" and the world, and between "John" and "Debbie."

But this separation exists only in the mind. The mind is projecting an illusion of separation, just as a movie projector casts images onto a screen. In reality, the screen remains unchanged and unaffected by the images that appear on it. Similarly, awareness remains whole and undivided, regardless of the temporary identities and experiences that arise within it.

To say that we are "disconnected" from universal awareness is itself part of the illusion. It presupposes that there are two separate objects: awareness on one side and the individual on the other. But in truth, there is no separation. The awareness IS the individual, whether they are conscious of it or not. The only difference is whether one recognizes this truth or remains veiled by the mental concept of separation.

Suffering: The Consequence of Misidentification

Suffering arises when universal awareness seemingly identifies with the psychological self and, in doing so, takes on the limitations of that psychological self or personal identity. When we believe we are "John" or "Debbie" or any other individual identity, we automatically adopt the fears, desires, and limitations associated with that identity. The body ages, the mind becomes anxious, circumstances change—and all of this IS the experience of suffering, because we believe that "I" am the individual person experiencing these things.

Again, this suffering IS the illusion of separation. The moment we see through the mental veil of personal identity and recognize that our true nature is the formless, already whole, complete, timeless awareness, we realize that psychological suffering cannot touch our essential being, even physical suffering, although varying degrees of pain are inevitable. Just as the sky remains untouched by the clouds that pass through it, so too does awareness remain unaffected by the transient experiences of the psychological self and body.

The Misconception of Reconnection

A common idea in spiritual practice is the notion of "reconnection"—the idea that we must reconnect with our true-self, with the source, or with the universe. But this idea implies and assumes that there is a real disconnection to begin with, that we have somehow been separated from the whole. In reality, there is no disconnection because there was never a separation to begin with. It is only the apparent psychological self or personal identity that seems to eclipse the underlying reality—like being born with tinted sunglasses that you leave on for your entire life. Therefore, never being able to experience the beauty of the natural world with the naked eye. In that sense, until we remove our sunglasses or somehow dissolve ego, our perspectives of ourselves, the world, and reality remain distorted, masked.

The concept of reconnection is based on the illusion that there are two separate objects—awareness on one side, and the individual on the other. But as we have seen, the individual is simply a projection of awareness, a temporary form arising within the formless. To say we need to "reconnect" is like saying that a wave needs to reconnect with the ocean or the boogeyman under the bed needs to reconnect with his source. The wave IS the ocean, just as universal awareness IS the individual. And the boogeyman is nothing but an idea or thought in the mind. There is no need to reconnect because there is no real individual or separation. Again, in the same way there is no boogeyman upon examining under the bed. Look within the body and see if you can find the person, psychological self, person identity YOU are innocently and mistakenly believing YOU are.

Recognizing Our True Nature

Instead of thinking in terms of "reconnection," it is more accurate to speak of recognition. The spiritual journey or path of enlightenment is not about reuniting two separate entities; it is more about shedding layers of delusional beliefs we hold about ourselves, life, others, and reality; more about recognizing that we were never separate to begin with; because there is no WE, no ME, only thisherenow—awareness. Awareness is always present, always whole, always free, inseparable. The personal identity we carry—whether it is John or Debbie or anyone else—is a temporary veil that can fall away the moment we realize the deeper truth of our being.

Although the recognition of awareness being aware of itSELF is occurring more often than we realize, in practical terms, this recognition seems to be sped up through practices like meditation, contemplation, various other sacred processes, or simply reflecting on the nature of consciousness. When the mind quiets down, the veil of personal identity may thin, allowing a glimpse of the timeless, formless awareness that is our true nature.

There Is Only One Reality

The notion of separation and that there is a solid person experiencing are illusions created by the mind—just thoughts. We are not separate nor are we solid beings disconnected from universal awareness. Rather, we are awareness itself, temporarily experiencing life through the veil of personal identity. In fact, upon investigation we discover that the "body" is merely a culmination of fluid non solid sensations constantly in motion arising from permanent unchanging reality.

Whether it appears as "John" or "Debbie" or anyone else, the ultimate reality remains the same, unchanging. There is no separation between individuals, nor between the individual and the deeper reality of existence, yet only in fleeting appearance. Of course, all of us are diverse in appearance and expression BUT NOT separate, NOT solid, NOT the mental energy called ego we are pretending to be.

Instead of seeking to reconnect with something outside ourselves, the key lies in recognizing that we have always been one with and as universal awareness—the timeless, formless reality that is the essence of all life. Suffering arises only when we forget this truth and identify with the fleeting experiences of the mind and body. By seeing through the illusion of separation (which is more psychological), and illusion of solidity (which is more of a feeling misinterpretation), we can return to the peace and clarity of knowing our true, undivided and non solid intangible nature.

End of Chapter Wisdom

Dissolving the illusion of separation starts with recognizing our connectedness with all life. Try a daily oneness meditation: sit quietly and reflect on how each person, object, or experience in your life is part of the same awareness that animates you. Another helpful practice is compassionate observation: when you encounter others, mentally acknowledge, "We are not separate," and notice how this shifts your perceptions. Through these practices, the illusion of separation begins to fade, unveiling the unity and wholeness that is our true nature.

Beyond the veil exists infinite
~ Abundance ~

— Chapter 23 —

The Path to Liberation: Realizing the True-Self Beyond Illusion

This chapter guides us along the path to liberation, uncovering the realization of the true-self that lies beyond the illusions created by the mind. By seeing through these layers of false identity and limiting beliefs, we awaken to our true nature as pure awareness—boundless, peaceful, and free. This journey of self-discovery is one of surrendering illusions and stepping into the deeper truth of who we really are.

Throughout human history, sages, mystics, and spiritual teachers have pointed to a profound truth: the way out of suffering lies in realizing the inseparable nature of our being. This realization is known by many names across different traditions—God-Realization, Self-Realization, Enlightenment, Christ-Consciousness, Buddha-Nature, Krishna-Consciousness, and others. Though the terminology varies, they all point to the same essential truth: the recognition of our birthless, deathless self, which exists prior to the formation of the personal identity or psychological self.

This chapter explores how spiritual practices such as meditation, yoga, and self-inquiry can help dissolve the illusion of the separate self and allow the universal reality to become aware of itself. Just as figures like the Buddha, Jesus Christ, Krishna, and Adiyogi realized their inseparable reality, we too can experience life from a perspective beyond personal identity, seeing all beings and all things as part of the One Self.

The Illusion of the Separate Self

At the heart of suffering is the ego—the personal identity or psychological self. This ego is built upon a collection of thoughts, memories, and concepts that create the illusion of separation. The ego tells us that "I am this body, I am this mind, I am this individual," and everything outside of this self becomes "other." This duality—of self and other—when identified with—is ultimately the source of all suffering, such as fear, desire, attachment, aversion, clinging, worry, stress, anxiety, and so forth. Again, the key is to dance and play in the divine theatre of duality—experience. Just do not mistake it for "myself."

However, as previously described, this separate self is no more real than the boogeyman under the bed. Just as a child might be convinced that the boogeyman is lurking in the shadows, the mind projects the illusion of the ego, making it seem real. But when you truly look for the boogeyman, you find nothing there. The boogeyman was never real to begin with—it was simply a creation of the mind, born from fear and misunderstanding.

The ego operates in a similar way. It tries to protect itself, constantly seeking validation, comfort, and improvement. It wants to feel secure, to be in control, to become something better. But just like the boogeyman, the ego is an illusion. It does not exist in reality; it is a mental projection. The moment we recognize this, we can begin to dissolve the ego and free ourselves from its grasp.

The Way Out of Suffering

The way out of suffering, then, is not to improve the ego or to make it feel better, but to see through the illusion of the ego entirely. The answer is to look for the ego—just as you would look for the boogeyman under the bed. When you search for the separate self, you will find that it does not exist as an independent entity. It is simply fleeting thoughts, concepts, feelings, and sensations looping in the mind as mostly beliefs arising and fading away in awareness, but it has no substance of its own. Try this: Point right now to where you are in the Body. Where do you point? Is there a pause of uncertainty? That's how we know we are not the body, not the mind.

This process of looking within is central to many spiritual paths. Practices such as meditation, self-inquiry, and yoga provide a means of dissolving the psychological self, revealing the birthless, deathless reality that lies beneath. When the ego falls away, what remains is the ONLY True Universal SELF—the formless, timeless inseparable awareness. Again, it is only our projection of separateness as seen through the egoic perspective of "me-ness" as a personal identity or psychological self, that makes it seem like YOU are fundamentally different from anyone else; or anything for that matter.

Sacred Processes for Realization

Throughout the ages, various spiritual traditions have developed sacred processes to help individuals realize their true nature. These practices are not about improving the ego but about transcending it entirely. Some of the most well-known practices include:

Meditation: In meditation, the mind is quieted, and the attention is turned inward. Through stillness and observation, one can begin to see the fleeting nature of thoughts, emotions, and sensations. As the mind quiets, the illusion of the separate self dissolves, and awareness recognizes itself as the timeless, formless reality.

Self-Inquiry: A practice popularized by sages like Ramana Maharshi, self-inquiry involves asking the fundamental question, "Who am I?" By persistently inquiring into the nature of the self, one can see through the false identities of the ego and realize the deeper, universal awareness that underlies all experience. We inquire any number of ways by investigating inwardly into the body and mind to become aware if what we believe is actually true; if who I believe myself to be can be found.

Yoga: More than just physical postures, yoga is a system of spiritual practice aimed at union with the divine, as the divine itSELF. Through the discipline of the body, mind, and breath, especially Kriya Yoga practitioners can move beyond the identification with the body and mind, realizing their oneness with the universal consciousness.

Contemplation: Contemplative practices involve deep reflection on spiritual truths and the nature of existence. By contemplating the teachings of enlightened masters or sacred texts, one can cultivate insight into the nature of reality and the illusory nature of the ego.

These practices are all methods for dissolving the false self and coming into the seeming direct contact with the universal reality as reality—or being aware of being aware. When practiced with sincerity and dedication, they lead to the realization that there is no separation—that the individual self is merely a temporary form, and the ultimate reality is the timeless, formless awareness that underlies all things.

Realization of Universal Consciousness

As the illusion of the separate self dissolves, something extraordinary happens: the universe becomes aware of itself. In moments of realization, awareness recognizes its own nature. Just as the Buddha, Jesus Christ, Krishna, and Adiyogi experienced, the individual remains, but not as a limited body-mind complex. Rather, the individual is seen from the universal perspective, where everything—every being, every object, every experience—is understood as part of the One Self.

In this state of realization, the individual no longer operates from the perspective of separation. They see themselves not as an isolated ego, but as an expression of the infinite, formless consciousness. The physical body and mind continue to exist, but they are no longer seen as the "self." Instead, the true-self is recognized as the universal awareness that permeates all things. This is the essence of God-Realization, Self-Realization, and Enlightenment—the recognition that there is only One Self.

Freedom from Fear and Suffering

Just as the child is freed from the fear of the boogeyman once they realize there is no monster under the bed, we are freed from the suffering of the ego once we recognize that the separate self does not exist. The illusion of separation, which is the root of fear, anxiety, and suffering, dissolves in the light of this realization.

The answer to overcoming the fear of the ego and the suffering it creates is to look for it. When we search for the separate self—when we investigate the ego and ask, "Who am I really?"—we find that it has no solid foundation. It is simply a mirage created by the mind. In seeing through this mirage, we become free from its power. The fear of the boogeyman evaporates the moment we shine a light under the bed, and the fear of the ego dissolves when we look deeply into its nature and discover that it does not exist.

The One Self Beyond Illusion

Ultimately, the path to liberation is not about improving the ego or "fixing" the separate self. It is about seeing through the illusion of separation and realizing that we have always been one with and as universal consciousness. Through sacred processes like meditation, yoga, and self-inquiry, we can dissolve the false identities that veil the true nature of reality.

When the ego falls away, we awaken to the birthless, deathless self that is inseparable from the universe, because IT IS THE UNIVERSE. As this realization, we see all beings and all things as expressions of the One Self, and we experience life from the perspective of wholeness, freedom, and peace. Just as the boogeyman never existed, the separate self never existed either—both are illusions of the mind. The truth is that we are, and always have been, the infinite awareness that is the ground of all existence.

End of Chapter Wisdom

Liberation unfolds as we recognize the true-self beyond illusion. Begin this journey with self-inquiry, asking questions like, "Who am I beyond my thoughts and roles?" and simply observing without attachment. Another valuable practice is mindful release: when you notice attachment to beliefs or identities, consciously let them go, returning to a state of openness. Through these practices, the layers of illusion fall away, allowing the true-self—pure awareness—to emerge naturally.

Embrace your Superpower of
~ Observation ~

— Chapter 24 —

Egoic Tricks: How the Ego Hijacks Spirituality

This chapter examines the subtle ways in which the ego hijacks spirituality, using spiritual ideas and practices to reinforce its own sense of identity and superiority. Despite seeking truth, the ego may latch onto spiritual achievements, knowledge, or roles, creating a "spiritual ego" that masks true awakening. By recognizing these egoic tricks, we can stay grounded in authentic spiritual growth, free from the illusions of superiority or specialness

The ego, the part of the mind that creates a sense of separation and personal identity, is incredibly clever. It is, in fact, the greatest trickster we will ever encounter. Even in the pursuit of spirituality, enlightenment, and self-realization, the egoic mind finds ways to weave itself into the process, often making claims such as, "I see everything as myself," or "I see the divine in everyone." These may sound like the statements of someone who has reached spiritual realization, but they often reflect the ego's tricks—a subtle hijacking of spirituality itself.

The truth is, there is a profound difference between true realization and what we might call conceptualized realization—an intellectual understanding that hasn't yet penetrated the deeper layers of being. In this chapter, we will explore how the ego cleverly disguises itself in spiritual language and claims, how a truly realized being does not even hold concepts of "separation" or "inseparability" in the mind, and how this understanding can help discern the egoic tricks from true self-realization.

The Ego's Clever Disguise: Spirituality as a Tool

At its core, the ego's function is to preserve the sense of a separate, individual self. As long as the ego identifies with a body-mind complex—believing "I am this person"—it seeks to maintain control, importance, and survival. However, when the individual begins to pursue spiritual growth, the ego does not simply disappear. Instead, it often adapts, transforming itself into a spiritual ego.

The spiritual ego is a more subtle and sophisticated version of the ordinary ego. It uses the language of enlightenment, awakening, and divine realization, claiming things like, "I see everything as part of the one reality," or "I have realized that we are all divine." These statements, while they may sound lofty and enlightened, often come from a place of conceptual understanding, not from direct realization that is deeply abiding.

The spiritual ego operates by cloaking itself in conceptual knowledge and false humility (not true wisdom), making it more difficult to detect. Although most enlightened beings and awakened masters can talk for hours on the nature of reality and spiritual awakening, spiritual ego can talk endlessly about non-duality, oneness, and universal consciousness as well, but all the while, it remains entrenched in the illusion of separation. It subtly takes credit for being more "spiritually advanced" than others, claiming an elevated status through its intellectual grasp of spiritual truths.

True Realization vs. Conceptual Realization

True realization is not an intellectual achievement. It is a direct and experiential recognition of the inseparable nature of reality—a state in which the personal identity falls away, and the underlying universal awareness reveals itself. This kind of realization is beyond concepts like "oneness" or "separation." It is a lived experience where distinctions no longer make sense, and where the mind rests in its natural state of silence and knowing.

In contrast, although true glimpses of reality or universal awareness often occur, ego quickly claims the short-lived realization for itself, thereby remaining lost in the conceptual realization as an intellectual understanding of these truths. The ego-mind grasps the ideas of non-separation, oneness, and the nature of reality, but it has not yet fully internalized them because that means dissolving itself. The individual may understand the concepts of spiritual teachings from mere glimpses and even teach them to others, but the deep, direct realization is not yet present. Once more, the ego can easily hijack those true glimpses and turn them into conceptual realizations, making it into a tool for reinforcing its own sense of existence, importance, and often, spiritual superiority.

Herein lies the key difference:

A being who has truly realized their inseparable reality does not even hold the concept of separation or inseparability in their mind. They rarely, if ever, say things like, "I see everything as myself," because from the perspective of true realization, there is no "I" that sees and no "everything" to be seen. These distinctions vanish in the light of experience that is deeply abiding.

On the other hand, a person operating from conceptual realization or ego hijacking of true glimpses might frequently talk about non-duality, oneness, and how "everything is divine," because the ego still clings to these ideas as a way of reinforcing its own identity.

The Realized Being and the Egoic Trick

Only a truly realized master, or a deeply enlightened being, can discern this egoic trick in others. It is subtle, but the difference between genuine realization and egoic imitation is as profound as the difference between seeing and thinking about seeing.

For a realized being, the experience of unity is so natural and effortless that there is no need to proclaim it. They live from a place of direct, unspoken knowing. They see the world not as separate individuals, but as an indivisible whole. They understand that words can never capture the essence of this realization, so they rarely feel the need to explain or describe it. As the saying goes: "The one who sees cannot say, and the one who says cannot know."

This phrase captures the essence of the egoic trick. A person who feels the need to continually assert their spiritual insight is likely still caught in the web of the ego, operating from conceptual understanding. True realization is silent, humble, and beyond the need for such proclamations.

Similarly: "The one who speaks does not know, and the one who knows does not speak."

In the same way, someone who continually talks about their spiritual achievements or insights may not yet have reached the depth of genuinely full realization. The one who truly knows does not feel the need to explain or justify their experience because their knowing is direct and beyond words.

The Ego as the Boogeyman

The ego, like the boogeyman under the bed, does not actually exist in the way we think it does. Just as a child believes in the boogeyman despite there being no evidence of its existence, the mind creates the illusion of the separate self as a solid tangible entity—the ego—even though it has no real, independent substance.

The ego's efforts to improve itself, to become more spiritual, to feel better, or to attain enlightenment are part of its own illusory game. In fact, ultimately, the spiritual journey is actually the ego's journey. (That last sentence will make sense sooner or later.) It is constantly trying to make itself more significant and figure out life and expereince, all while reinforcing the very separation it is trying to overcome. This is the ultimate egoic trick: ego convinces itself that it can attain enlightenment, when in reality, enlightenment is the dissolution of the ego itself—ego death—the end of yourself as you believe yourself to be—the end of your world.

So, how do we become free of the fear of the ego or the boogeyman? How do we escape this illusion? The answer is simple, yet profound: look for it while questioning if our thoughts and beliefs are absolutely true for providing the everlasting peace and sense of self we are seeking. We also allow our minds to accept everything as it is—allowing all experience to be as it is, feelings, thoughts, sensations from the most loving and happy to the most painful and terrifying—to be exactly as they are herenow.

Just as a child shines a light under the bed to reveal that the boogeyman is not real, we must look for the ego. When we search for the separate self, we discover that it does not exist as an independent entity. It is simply a collection of thoughts, beliefs, conditioned responses, and fleeting sensations of energy in motion—nothing more. The moment we see through the illusion, the fear and attachment to the ego idea begins to dissolve.

Beyond the Egoic Tricks

Redundantly speaking, the egoic mind is the greatest trickster, even in the realm of spirituality. It uses concepts of oneness, non-duality, and enlightenment to maintain its grip on our sense of self. But true realization is beyond concepts. It is a direct experience of inseparable reality, a stateless state in which the mind no longer clings to ideas of separation or unity. A realized being does not feel the need to proclaim their insight, for they live it silently and naturally.

The ego, like the boogeyman, is an illusion that vanishes when we shine the light of awareness on it. The key is to look for it, to investigate the nature of the separate self—to see if you can actually find the solid inner self you believe you are; and in doing so, discover that it has no actual tangible substance in the way we belief it does. Remember: You are not the body and not even the mind but something deeper, spontaneous, always herenow, no matter what the mind says about experience. True freedom comes not from improving the ego or spiritualizing it, but from seeing through its illusions entirely.

As previously stated:

"The one who sees cannot say, and the one who says cannot know."

The path to self-realization lies not in speaking about the truth, but in effortlessly being the truth without force, in living from the direct, wordless recognition of our inseparable reality.

End of Chapter Wisdom

True spirituality is about transcending the ego, not feeding it. To stay aware of the ego's influence, practice humble self-reflection: regularly ask, "Am I using spirituality to feel superior or special?" and be honest with yourself. Another helpful practice is silent presence—spend time each day in meditation without striving for insights or achievements, allowing yourself to simply be. Through these practices, we can let go of egoic tricks, deepening our spiritual journey with genuine openness and humility.

When in doubt, remember this:
~ Gratitude Heals ~

— Chapter 25 —

The Survival System and Awareness: Navigating Human Existence

This chapter explores the egoic survival system and how it operates within awareness in our everyday lives. The ego functions as a protective mechanism, focused on maintaining the physical self and navigating the demands of survival, while awareness represents our deeper, unchanging nature. By understanding the role of ego and changeless awareness, we can navigate human existence with greater balance, allowing our true-self to guide us rather than reactive patterns.

While we live and function as human beings, we experience reality through two fundamental qualities: the Survival System and Awareness. The Survival System consists of the body and the mind, which work together to ensure physical safety and survival. On the other hand, Awareness is the deeper, formless consciousness that lies beyond the mind and body—the universal awareness that transcends personal identity and concepts.

This chapter will explore the roles of these two qualities, how the mind functions as a navigational tool for survival, and how the ego, as part of the mind, creates the illusion of a separate "self." Understanding the distinction between the Survival System and Awareness helps us navigate life with clarity, recognizing the ego's limitations while deepening our connection to the formless awareness that is our true nature.

The Survival System: Body and Mind

At the most practical level, the Survival System ensures that the human body can continue to function and thrive in the physical world. It consists of two key components:

The Body: The physical vessel through which experience occurs. The body is equipped with senses, muscles, organs, and systems that allow us to interact with and respond to the environment. The body ensures survival by managing basic needs like hunger, thirst, and physical safety.

The Mind: The mind serves as the navigational system of the body, processing sensory information, interpreting situations, and making decisions. Its primary function is to keep the body out of harm's way and ensure that we continue to survive in various environments.

The mind itself can be further divided into several aspects:

- Intellect: The faculty of reasoning and analysis. The intellect helps us solve problems, plan for the future, and make decisions based on logic and facts.
- Memory: Memory allows us to store and retrieve past experiences, which helps us learn from previous situations and avoid repeating mistakes. Without memory, we would struggle to survive because we wouldn't remember what is harmful or beneficial.
- Imagination: Imagination enables us to visualize future scenarios and possibilities, helping us anticipate potential dangers or opportunities. It is crucial for creativity and innovation but also for planning and preparing for survival-related tasks.
- Ego: The ego is an abstraction created by the mind to make sense of experiences. It is the part of the mind that identifies with the body and the personal story of "me" or "I." While the ego serves a functional role in navigating the world, it also creates the illusion of separation.

The Ego: An Abstraction of the Mind

At its core, the ego is a mental construct that helps the mind organize experience around the idea of a personal self. It identifies with the body, thoughts, and life story, creating a sense of individuality. For example, the ego says, "I am this person," or "I am John, who was born in this place, who has had these experiences." The ego filters experiences through the lens of personal identity, reinforcing the idea that "I" am separate from others and the world around me.

However, this sense of "I" is not inherently real. It is a mental abstraction designed to help navigate the practical aspects of life. The ego helps us distinguish "my body" from "other bodies" so that we can avoid danger, protect ourselves, and make choices that sustain life. For instance, when crossing a street, the ego prompts you to think, "I need to be careful to avoid being hit by a car." In this way, the ego is useful for survival.

Yet, the problem arises when the ego's conceptual self—this idea of "me"—is mistaken for our true-self. The egoic mind begins to take on the false persona of a separate self, constantly seeking validation, protection, and improvement. It identifies with external achievements, relationships, and even spiritual practices, reinforcing the illusion that "I" am distinct from others and the world.

For example, the ego might say, "I am smarter than others," or "I need to succeed to feel valuable," or even, "I am more spiritual than others because I meditate every day." These are all examples of the ego attaching itself to roles, ideas, and comparisons, which create a false sense of separation and can lead to feelings of superiority, inferiority, or insecurity.

The Illusion of Separation

The sense of separation created by the ego is a false persona, a mental veil that obscures the deeper truth of who we are. In reality, the "I" that the ego projects is simply a collection of thoughts, memories, and concepts. It is not our true-self. Our true nature is the awareness—pure presence that never leaves—that lies behind all thoughts, experiences, and identities—a timeless, formless consciousness that cannot be limited by the body or the mind.

An example of this illusion of separation can be seen in social interactions. Imagine you are in a group setting, and your ego might begin comparing itself to others: "Am I more successful than them?" "Do they think I'm interesting?" "I need to say something impressive." These thoughts arise from the ego's sense of being separate, constantly evaluating itself against others to maintain its identity. But this comparison is based on a false sense of self—the idea that "I" am this separate individual, distinct from the whole.

In truth, the awareness that underlies your experience is the same awareness that underlies everyone's experience. The separation exists only in the mind, created by the ego's insistence on seeing itself as separate from the world. The same consciousness is flowing through all beings; it is only the mind that creates distinctions like "me" and "you."

Awareness: The True-Self

While the Survival System is essential for navigating the world and ensuring physical well-being, awareness is the deeper, universal consciousness that exists beyond the mind and body. This awareness is the true-self—the formless, timeless presence that remains constant, even as the body and mind undergo change.

Imagine a clear sky with clouds passing through it. The clouds represent thoughts, memories, and experiences, while the sky represents awareness itself. The clouds come and go, but the sky remains unchanged. Similarly, awareness remains constant and untouched, regardless of the changing experiences that arise within it. Place your full attention on this spaceless presence. Allow your attention to abide in this pure awareness. As this non mental awareness, the mind and all experience is noticed, but not claimed as, "This is me."

Unlike the ego, awareness does not identify with the body or mind. It is simply the observer, witnessing all thoughts, sensations, and actions without attachment. Awareness does not get caught up in concepts of "I" or "me." It does not need to protect or defend itself because it is not separate from anything. It simply is—the background in which all experiences arise and dissolve.

The Harmony of Survival System and Awareness

Though the Survival System and Awareness seem to operate on different levels, they are not in opposition. The Survival System serves its purpose by keeping the body safe and functioning in the world, while Awareness is the deeper truth of our existence, guiding us beyond the illusions of the ego.

When we recognize the distinction between these two, we can allow the Survival System to do its job without getting caught in the ego's tricks. For example, you can navigate the world, make decisions, and ensure your well-being without identifying with the false persona of the ego. You can see thoughts like "I need to impress them" as simply part of the mind's function, without believing that they define who you are. In fact, as every Awakened Master has been saying for the last 15 thousand years: Thought has no inherent reality.

In practical terms, this means living with a deeper awareness that transcends the mind while still allowing the mind and body to function naturally. You can allow thought to be as it is without believing them; hence, you can engage in daily activities, work, relationships, and challenges from a place of clarity, knowing that the true-self is not the separate "I" that the ego projects but the universal awareness in which all experiences unfold.

Navigating Life with Clarity

In summary, human existence is supported by what seems to be two complementary systems,: the Survival System and Awareness; although awareness is inseparable and the survival process arises in it, from it. The Survival System consists of the body and mind, including the ego, which functions as a tool for navigating the practical aspects of life. The ego, while useful for survival, creates the illusion of separation by identifying with the false persona of "me" or "I." Ironically, we could say that the reason ego arises is because ego is suffering and suffering is ego, which creates an invitation to consciously embark on the spiritual journey—to be free from suffering, to be free from itself. In that sense, suffering pushes us to be free from it by seeking our ultimate reality. That is the temporary gift of suffering leading to the permanent realization of everlasting joyous appreciation and love, when we look.

Furthermore, beyond the mind and body lies awareness—the true-self that is birthless, deathless, and inseparable from the whole. By recognizing the ego's tricks and illusions, we can live in harmony with both the Survival System and Awareness, allowing the mind to function as a tool while resting in the deeper truth of our inseparable, universal nature.

End of Chapter Wisdom

Finding harmony between the survival instincts of the ego and the presence of awareness is key to navigating life consciously. Practice mindful observation by noticing when you are reacting from a survival mindset and gently bring your focus back to the present. Another useful exercise is grounding in awareness: throughout the day, pause and recognize that beyond thoughts and fears, there is a still awareness within you. By regularly reconnecting with this awareness, you empower yourself to live from a place of clarity and balance.

Prior to experience is timeless abiding

~ Presence ~

— Chapter 26 —

The Ultimate Freedom: Surrendering the Egoic Self to Universal Intelligence

This chapter explores the concept of ultimate freedom as the act of surrendering the egoic self to Universal Intelligence. Letting go of the ego's need for control and self-preservation allows us to live in alignment with a higher, unchanging awareness. In surrendering to this universal intelligence, we discover a profound inner freedom, trusting in life's natural flow rather than striving to control it.

The pursuit of freedom has been a central theme in human existence for millennia. However, the ultimate freedom is not the freedom to act according to our desires or will, but rather the freedom from the bondage of the egoic self. This freedom comes from recognizing that the ego, which operates through the limited intelligence of the body-mind, is not who we truly are. The ego, with its accumulation of data, ideas, and personal identity, is a construct—a mental abstraction designed to help us navigate the world, but it limits us from experiencing the deeper, universal intelligence underneath everything.

In this chapter, we will explore the idea of surrendering the personal will to the universal will, how this brings true freedom, and how sacred processes used for millennia help individuals wake up from the dream of ego-hood or personhood, leading to the realization of their true nature.

The Limited Intelligence of the Egoic Self

The egoic self operates on the programmed intelligence of the body-mind. This intelligence is built up over a lifetime, consisting of thoughts, memories, conditioning, and accumulated knowledge. It also includes one's natural intellectual abilities, emotional tendencies, and psychological proclivities. This is the personal intelligence—shaped by upbringing, education, societal norms, and life experiences.

For example, if someone has been raised in an environment that values competition and success, their personal intelligence will likely develop tendencies toward ambition, comparison, and the drive for achievement. They might identify strongly with their career or social status, thinking, "I am successful because of my hard work, my intellect, and my accomplishments." This identification with personal achievements and capabilities becomes part of the egoic self—the false sense of "I" that feels separate from the rest of the world.

The ego, however, is inherently limited. It operates on accumulated data and memory, and it is deeply influenced by the past and conditioned responses. While it can navigate the practical aspects of life, it is confined to the realm of personal will—the idea that "I" must control, manage, and direct everything in life. This sense of control gives the ego a sense of importance and purpose, but it is also the source of its bondage. The ego's need for control, validation, and survival keeps it locked in a cycle of fear, desire, and separation from the deeper reality of existence.

Universal Intelligence: Beyond the Personal Mind

Beyond the limited personal intelligence of the body-mind is a vast, universal intelligence—a formless, timeless source of wisdom and insight that exists beyond individual thought and memory. This intelligence is the same universal awareness that permeates all of existence. It is the intelligence that guides the growth of a tree, orchestrates the flow of the universe, and underlies the natural order of life.

To access this universal intelligence, one must move beyond the interference of the personal identity or egoic mind. This process involves surrendering the personal will to the universal will—allowing life to flow through us, as us, rather than trying to force or control outcomes based on the ego's limited perspective. When we surrender the egoic self, we open ourselves to a deeper intelligence that can guide us with far greater clarity, wisdom, and peace.

An example of this can be seen in moments of deep creativity or flow. Imagine a musician who is completely immersed in playing an instrument. In these moments, they are not thinking about themselves, their abilities, or the outcome of their performance. They have surrendered the need to control and are simply allowing the music to flow through them. In this state, they are tapping into universal intelligence—a creative force that goes beyond the limitations of the personal mind.

Similarly, when an athlete is "in the zone," they are no longer operating from the egoic mind. The body moves effortlessly, and the mind is silent. In these moments, the individual is aligned with universal intelligence—they are not acting from a place of "I am doing this," but rather, "this is happening through me—as me." Ultimately, there is no separate doer, no separate me, or a separate doing, but only what is, only what is happening. And poetically speaking, the ultimate surrender is becoming aware that the dance and dancer are inseparably one—that the you YOU have believed yourself to be has never done anything; that it was nothing more or less than the universe unfolding through what seemed to be a separate person or individual as filtered through the fantasies and imaginings of the egoic mind.

Surrendering the Personal Will to the Universal Will

Surrender is the key to accessing universal intelligence. To surrender the personal will means to let go of the ego's need to control, manage, and direct life. In a way, surrender also means not "doing" anything or absolutely allowing everything to be as it is. In that sense, it means trusting that there is a deeper intelligence that knows what is best and allowing this intelligence to inform our actions, decisions, and experiences beyond the trappings of egoic decision making lost in rationalizations, justifications, and inner negotiations.

In practical terms, surrender looks like letting go of rigid attachments to specific outcomes. For instance, rather than insisting, "I need this job to be happy," or "I must achieve this goal to feel successful," or "This person must like me in order for me to feel worthy," surrendering the personal will means trusting that whatever happens is part of a larger, intelligent reality—while becoming aware of your inherent, natural worthiness wholeness that is always here. It also means acting with clarity and intention beyond relentless talking to oneself (inner negotiations) but releasing the egoic attachment to how things must unfold.

This surrender is not passive; it is an active alignment with the flow of life. It requires deep trust, patience, and a willingness to move beyond the ego's demands for security and control. In doing so, we allow universal intelligence (that some call God or Cosmic Consciousness) to guide us, often in ways that are more harmonious, effective, and liberating than the ego could ever imagine.

Sacred Processes for Awakening

For millennia, sacred processes have been used to help individuals wake up from the dream of ego-hood or personhood. These practices are designed to dissolve the egoic mind and allow for the direct experience of universal intelligence and awareness. Some of the most well-known processes are included below and specific resources and methods can be found at www.discoverCHA.org or merely searching for them on the internet:

Meditation: By quieting the mind and withdrawing attention from the constant stream of thoughts and identification with the ego, meditation allows the deeper reality of universal awareness to emerge—reality that has always been here now. In meditation, one can experience the stillness and spaciousness of being beyond the personal mind, aligning more fully with universal intelligence; ultimately becoming aware that one is the universe itSELF. Aware of being aware. *Suggested Teachers*: Adyashanti, Gangaji, Mooji, Father Thomas Keating (centering prayer)

Yoga: Beyond the physical postures, yoga is a spiritual practice that seeks to dissolve the illusory veil of separation projecting that the individual is separate from the universal. Through disciplined practice of the body, breath, and mind, yoga helps dissolve the egoic sense of separateness, allowing for a direct sense of universal awareness. *Suggested Teachers*: Sadhguru

Self-Inquiry: A process of asking, "Who am I?" to peel away the layers of identification with the body, mind, and ego. Through self-inquiry, one can directly experience the truth that the egoic self is an illusion, revealing the universal intelligence that is always present. *Suggested Teachers*: Rupert Spira, Byron Katie, Eckhart Tolle

Surrender Practices: Many spiritual traditions encourage practices of surrender, where one consciously lets go of personal desires and outcomes, trusting the flow of life and the guidance of universal intelligence. These practices help dissolve the ego's need for control, opening the individual to a deeper sense of freedom. *Suggested Teacher:* David Hawkins, MD, PHD

The Example of Waking Up from Ego

To illustrate this concept of waking up from the dream of ego, consider the experience of someone who has lived their entire life identifying with their career. They believe, "I am a doctor," or "I am a successful businessperson," and their sense of self-worth is tightly bound to this identity. Every decision they make is driven by the need to maintain this identity, to prove themselves, and to succeed. And, without that identity they feel unworthy, useless, not good enough.

Now, imagine that this person begins to engage in meditation and self-inquiry. Over time, they start to see that their sense of identity and worthiness as "a doctor" or "a businessperson" is just a role they play in the world. It is not who they truly are. As they deepen their practice, they begin to realize that beyond their job, beyond their achievements, there is a formless, timeless presence—the universal awareness that has always been there, silently observing—naturally and always whole, complete, enough, worthy.

This realization brings about a profound shift. The person no longer feels the need to cling to their career identity or prove themselves to others. Henceforth, egoic energies begin dissolving and falling away. They still perform their job, but now they do so with a sense of freedom—knowing that their true nature is not defined by any role or achievement. They have surrendered the personal will to the universal will, allowing life to flow through them without the interference of the egoic mind.

The True Freedom

In the essence of surrender—True Freedom, we move beyond the limitations of the personal mind and experience the flow of life from a place of profound freedom, peace, and clarity. The ego no longer holds our attention captive, and we align our focus with the infinite intelligence that permeates all of existence. This is the true freedom—the freedom of living as an expression of the universal will. To be in the world yet not of it.

Sacred processes like meditation, yoga, and self-inquiry have been used for millennia to help individuals wake up from the dream of ego-hood, leading to the direct realization of their true, inseparable nature.

End of Chapter Wisdom

True freedom lies in releasing the ego's grip and surrendering to the wisdom of Universal Intelligence. Begin with a daily surrender practice: reflect on areas of your life where you feel resistance, and consciously release the need for control, trusting in a greater intelligence. Another powerful exercise is silent receptivity—spend time each day in quiet meditation, allowing yourself to receive rather than direct or plan. These practices help us to embrace surrender, opening the door to a life guided by peace, trust, and inner freedom.

A Special Note

A significant part of freeing ourselves from the grip of the egoic mind is by allowing ourselves and the mind to let go of judgment, including judgment of egoic activity itself. The ego thrives on criticism and comparison, even when directed inward. It often tricks us into believing that judging ourselves is a form of self-improvement, but in reality, this creates a loop of guilt, shame, and self-condemnation that reinforces its hold. For example, if you notice yourself having an envious thought, the ego may immediately judge it as "bad" or "wrong," creating layers of internal conflict. Instead of falling into this trap, practice observing the thought without attaching judgment, recognizing it as a passing activity of the mind, not a reflection of your true self.

Similarly, when you catch yourself judging others or external situations, pause and remember that this judgment arises from conditioned patterns, not from the infinite awareness you truly are. By consciously seeing the innocent nature of judgment and allowing ourselves to release it, we break the ego's cycle of self-perpetuation through the energy of hate (self-hate), creating space for acceptance, peace, and clarity. In this non-judgmental possibility, we allow ourselves and others to simply be—to live in inner harmony as true freedom.

— Chapter 27 —

Realizing the Ultimate Truth: Trusting the Unknown

This chapter delves into the profound journey of realizing the ultimate truth by learning to trust the unknown. Embracing the unknown allows us to move beyond the limitations of the ego and conditioned beliefs, opening ourselves to the boundless nature of existence that we ALREADY are ALWAYS. By trusting what we cannot see or control, we align with the deeper intelligence of life and uncover a more expansive understanding of reality—of ourSELF.

At the heart of the journey to healing, feeling, awakening lies a profound and often overlooked power: the ability to trust the unknown. In a world where we are conditioned to rely on what we can see, hear, touch, taste, and smell, placing trust in something beyond the five senses may seem daunting, even impossible. Yet, it is through this act of trust—trusting in the formless, timeless reality that we cannot perceive with the mind or senses—that we unlock a power far greater than anything the material world can offer.

This infinite, formless reality—whether we call it God, universal awareness, or simply the unknown—is the source of all that exists. It is the ground of being, the silent presence behind every thought, every sensation, and every experience. The nothingness from which all experience of somethingness arises. To trust in this invisible reality is to trust in the essence of life itself, the one constant that never changes. But doing so requires something that seems counterintuitive: embracing our vulnerability.

Invulnerability Through Vulnerability

When we place our trust in the material world, we are always at risk of disappointment—suffering. The body ages, relationships change, circumstances are unpredictable, and what we cling to for security can be lost in an instant—more suffering. This leads to a life lived in fear and control; hence, we try to manipulate reality to keep ourselves safe and free from suffering; but true safety, everlasting fulfillment, and unconditional happiness remains elusive.

However, when we choose to trust what cannot be detected by the senses—the formless reality—we discover an invulnerability that paradoxically arises from our absolute vulnerability—the Grace of Awareness. By surrendering our need to control and by opening ourselves to the unknown, we align with the infinite intelligence that sustains the entire universe. In doing so, we move beyond the limitations of the egoic mind, which thrives on fear, and step into the flow of life itself.

To trust in the unknown is to trust that we are supported by something far greater than the mind can comprehend. It means trusting that even when we do not know how things will unfold, we are held by cosmic intelligence (intelligent grace) that has no beginning or end. In this surrender, we find a deep peace, knowing that we do not have to figure everything out on our own. We realize that life itself is guiding us, moment by moment, and that our true security lies not in controlling outcomes, but in trusting the flow.

Trusting Trust Itself

At the deepest level, to trust trust itself is to place our faith in the only reality that truly exists. This formless, timeless presence—what many traditions refer to as the divine or universal consciousness—is beyond concepts, beyond form, and beyond the limitations of the personal mind. When we trust this reality, we are not trusting in something external or separate from ourselves. We are trusting in the essence of our own being, in the truth of who we are.

This trust is not blind faith, nor is it passive. It is an active surrender, an opening to the vastness of existence beyond what the mind can know. By trusting trust itself, we align with the infinite power that flows through all things, allowing ourselves to be guided by a wisdom far beyond our personal will. This is where we find our true invulnerability—our true birthless deathless nature—not in trying to protect ourselves from life's uncertainties, but in fully embracing them, knowing that the formless reality we trust is the very fabric of existence itself.

In the end, this trust is the greatest act of freedom. It frees us from the illusion of separation, from the fear that arises from the ego's need for control, from the limitations of the five senses, and from the obsessions and compulsions of primal instincts. It allows us to live in harmony with the unknown, finding peace in the mystery of life—as the Mystery ITSELF. To trust trust itself is to trust the eternal presence—the mystery that has always been and will always be—the Universal Truth of oneSELF—the ONLY SELF. And in that trust, we discover the essence of our true nature—invulnerable, infinite, birthless, deathless, timeless, formless, free—free to be free or free to be bound.

End of Chapter Wisdom

Trusting the unknown invites us into a realm of limitless potential and inner peace that never left—that is always herenow—the reality of being. To cultivate this trust, practice letting go of certainty by embracing situations where outcomes are unclear, allowing them to unfold without resistance. Another practice is open-minded contemplation: spend a few minutes each day reflecting on the mystery of life and the possibility that not all answers are meant to be known. Through these practices, we gradually release the need for control and deepen our trust in the ultimate truth that lies beyond the mind's limitations—the Universal Heart of ALL that IS.

End of Book Wisdom

At the heart of awakening lies a simple yet profound truth: allowing everything to be as it is. This means embracing life without forcing change or resisting what unfolds. When we allow our experience to be as it is, we release the mind's need to judge, control, or shape reality to fit the ego's desires. Instead, we find a peaceful acceptance that brings clarity and frees us from the seemingly real, yet illusory suffering we are creating in the mind.

Ultimately essential is allowing yourself to be as you are—recognizing that your true nature and spontaneous direct experience needs no fixing or improvement. By fully accepting experience and ourSELF as nothing other than THIS MOMENT, we align with the flow of life and open to the wisdom of Universal Intelligence—Grace—The Cosmos—God—Source Essence of All Creation. In this surrender exists a profound liberation, where peace, happiness, and inner freedom arise naturally and effortlessly from within and without—as YOUniverse.

When all else fails, forgive and
~ Surrender ~

APPENDIX I

Ego: A Creation of the Nervous System

The nervous system is the body's central energetic framework, controlling nearly all bodily functions. At its core is the brain and spinal cord, which operate as a single, interconnected unit constantly communicating with the rest of the body. Together, these structures generate and sustain the flow of electrical impulses that keep the body active and responsive.

From this continuous flow of electrical energy, electromagnetic fields emerge, creating dynamic fields of perception that surround and interact with the nervous system. These electromagnetic fields form what we experience as the mind, an energetic component that transcends physical form. The brain-spinal cord unit serves as the tangible, physical foundation, while the electromagnetic field acts as the mental component—the flow of mental energy that gives rise to thought, perception, and emotion.

In this sense, the nervous system does not just relay sensory information; it actively generates the field of consciousness that allows for all experience. The electromagnetic field surrounding the nervous system is an energetic mirror of the brain's activity and is crucial in shaping what we think, feel, and perceive. This relationship between the physical nervous system and the energetic mind-field creates an interplay of physical and mental experience, the flow of energy giving rise to both tangible sensations and the vast landscape of human thought and perception.

The nervous system doesn't just manage bodily functions; it also acts as a powerful mechanism for interpreting and abstracting experiences. Through this process of abstraction and conceptualization, it creates the notion of a separate self, or the ego—the psychological identity we think of as "me." This sense of personal identity is not a fixed reality but a construct formed from countless mental strategies, concepts, and interpretations based on the nervous system's data processing arising from the mind-field.

When we try to pinpoint our personal identity, we inevitably find it elusive. This is because the egoic self is composed of mental abstractions—thoughts, memories, interpretations, and judgments derived from the nervous system's electromagnetic field (mind). This field is a dynamic, constantly shifting energetic current, so any "sense of self" formed by it is also fluid, changing as the field changes. The nervous system, through its interaction of brain and spinal cord, produces patterns that are mysteriously interpreted as "who I am," even though this interpretation is never fixed or truly substantial.

Example: The Case of Changing Self-Perceptions

Consider someone who goes through a significant life change, like a career shift. As this person contemplates their new path, their nervous system generates countless thoughts and emotional responses that are reflected in their electromagnetic field—the mind-field. They might cycle through various mental constructs such as "I am successful," "I am afraid of failure," or "I am uncertain." These self-perceptions may shift from day to day, or even moment to moment, depending on the nervous system's current state and the interpretations it abstracts from experiences.

In this way, their "self" appears to be constantly changing: one day they feel confident, the next anxious, the next inspired. When they search within for a stable sense of identity, they find that it cannot be grasped because it's essentially a series of constantly shifting energy as mental strategies, emotional responses, and shifting self-images—all of which are abstractions created by the nervous system's ongoing electrical activity. The egoic self is thus a set of adaptive responses to stimuli, not an actual, unchanging entity or personal self.

The Illusion of a Solid Self

This example highlights why, when we search for our seemingly "personal" identity, we end up finding a vast array of psychological data, mental labels, and shifting perceptions; but not who or what one essentially is. The nervous system is constantly interpreting and responding, giving rise to new configurations of thought and self-image as the electromagnetic field changes. What we call the "ego" is merely the mind's effort to unify these fluctuating patterns into something cohesive, creating the illusion of a fixed, separate, psychological self.

One of the most fundamental abstractions that the nervous system creates is the "I-thought"—the notion of "I" as a reference point within experience. This "I-thought" serves as a cognitive tool that simulates a distinction between "I," the experiencer, and "other," the experience. Through this lens, the nervous system creates a virtual divide, where every sensation, thought, and perception is categorized in relation to an "I" that seems to be at the center of it all. This abstract "I" becomes the root of our egoic sense of self, a mental landmark around which other ideas, beliefs, and identities accumulate.

The "I-thought" initiates the simulation of separation by suggesting that there is an independent entity observing and interacting with a separate world. For instance, the experience of "I feel happy" or "I am angry" implies that there is an "I" having an experience separate from the emotion or event. Over time, the nervous system builds on this distinction, layering thoughts and interpretations that reinforce the notion of "me" as a separate, individual entity navigating a world of separate "others."

This initial "I-thought" becomes the foundation of a vast network of self-referential thoughts and interpretations, ultimately producing a strong, consistent sense of ego or personal identity—a false self. Yet, this "I" is not a fixed reality; it is an abstract tool created by the nervous system to organize experiences, not an actual, unchanging self. By understanding the "I-thought" as a functional abstraction rather than a true self, we begin to see how our sense of separation and individuality is mentally constructed rather than innately real.

Ultimately, the personal identity or ego (me, myself, i) is an ever-changing mental construct, a fluid abstraction rooted in the nervous system's activity (mind). This is why true inner clarity comes from moving beyond the identification with these fluctuating self-images and understanding that our true nature is not the mental construct but the underlying Universal Awareness that observes it all—the unchanging permanent Reality from which all experience (everything) arises.

The Fleeting Experience of the Body as a Perception

The body, as we perceive it, is not a fixed, concrete entity but rather a constantly changing, impermanent experience generated by the nervous system. The nervous system continuously gathers and interprets sensory data—signals from organs, muscles, skin, and more—abstracting this information into a cohesive "body image" that we experience as our physical form. Once more, as a psychological creation. This perception of the body is a mental construct, a synthesized representation that allows us to relate to and make sense of our experiences. The body, in this sense, is an abstraction of sensory data that gives context and structure to what we experience, making it meaningful and coherent.

By creating this perceptual construct of the body, the nervous system provides a point of reference for our interactions and responses. For example, sensations of warmth, pressure, and movement are all processed and unified to create the perception of "my hand" or "my arm." This abstracted body image allows us to navigate the physical world in a way that feels grounded and tangible. However, this body is not static; it is an ever-shifting, dynamic experience—a moment-to-moment interpretation rather than a concrete form. It changes with our thoughts, emotions, physical states, and environmental conditions, revealing its impermanent and fluid nature.

This understanding shows that our sense of the body is a functional projection of sensory input rather than an unchanging reality. The nervous system constructs this perception to enable experience, interaction, and meaning. As we observe this process, we realize that the body, like all perceptions, is a temporary, adaptable abstraction created to provide context for experience—fundamentally allowing life to be experienced in a rich and organized way.

Ultimately, the reality of one's true SELF is the unchanging Universal Awareness that watches and observes the body, thoughts, and experiences. In truth, experience arises within YOU, as YOU—as the Universe itself—rather than the idea that you arise because of experience. In other words, YOU are not in the body, the body is in YOU. This Awareness is the constant, foundational universal presence that exists prior to any perception or sensation or experience of a body-mind complex. Experience may give rise to the idea of a personal self—the "I-thought," the "me-idea," and images of "myself"—but these concepts exist solely as tools for navigating life, not as personal identities to attach to. The "I" concept is a functional reference, a mental construct designed to organize experience, but it is not the true self. Recognizing this distinction allows us to live in freedom, as our true nature as Universal Awareness, beyond the transient labels and constructs of identity.

Suggested Exercise: Observing the Fleeting Nature of the Mind Through Meditation

In this meditation practice, you will turn your attention inward to directly observe the impermanent, ever-changing nature of thoughts, sensations, and experiences. With regular practice, this can reveal the illusion of a separate, finite self.

1. Find a Quiet Space: Sit comfortably in a quiet place, with your back upright and your body relaxed. Close your eyes and begin by taking a few deep breaths, allowing yourself to settle into stillness.
2. Turn Attention Inward: Once you feel centered, gently shift your attention inward. Rather than focusing on external sounds or sensations, bring awareness to the inner landscape of your mind. Notice any thoughts, images, or feelings that arise.
3. Observe Without Attachment: As thoughts or emotions come and go, simply observe them. Do not label or judge them as good or bad; instead, notice them as they are—temporary waves arising in the mind. Watch as each thought or sensation appears, lingers briefly, and then fades away.
4. Notice Impermanence: With each passing thought, feeling, or mental image, become aware of its impermanence. Notice that everything you experience internally is in constant motion, shifting from one moment to the next. See if you can observe these fluctuations without grasping or identifying with any single thought or emotion.
5. Return to Awareness: Whenever you feel yourself attaching to a thought or feeling, gently return to observing the awareness itself—the silent, unchanging witness of these experiences. Begin to sense the spaciousness in which all thoughts, sensations, and emotions arise and dissolve.
6. Recognize the Illusion of Self: Over time, or even in a single session, you may notice that the idea of a fixed "me" is simply

a series of thoughts and images arising in this spacious awareness. See if you can glimpse the freedom in realizing that your true nature is the unchanging awareness behind these fleeting experiences—not the temporary identities they suggest.

Practice this meditation regularly to strengthen your understanding that while the mind creates the illusion of a finite, separate self, your true self is the universal awareness observing it all.

APPENDIX II

About CHA

Collective Healing Anonymous (CHA) emerges as a groundbreaking non-religious, yet highly spiritual process and support group that goes beyond the limitations of traditional 12-step programs. Offering a fresh perspective rooted in collective consciousness and deep introspection, CHA offers a transformative path toward Self-Discovery, Healing, and everlasting Inner Freedom. CHA further provides the absolute potential to fully recover from any and all obsessions, compulsions, addictions, dependencies, and identity matters, in THIS LIFE! In short, Collective Healing Anonymous is a Revolutionary and Empowering Possibility to heal, feel, and awaken, together! www.discovercha.org

The CHA Basics Book

The CHA Basics book, in simple and relatable terms, shares CHA's foundational purpose, basic structure, and essential ingredients for fully understanding and participating in the CHA Process and Community. This guide also shares compassionate wisdom and guidance toward healing and awakening, what to expect when attending meetings, and the importance of including Sacred Processes in your life, as well as providing specific and easy to follow tips to begin living the life you know in your heart is possible. Lastly, detailed instructions about how to start and conduct a CHA gathering in your area are available in the Tool Box Section of this book.

Moving forward, to allow Collective Healing Anonymous to best work for you, it may be helpful to understand that CHA is not a belief system, philosophy, and not a religious teaching; does not ascribe to any single doctrine, guru, or spiritual master. It is, however, a supportive non-religious spiritual process and support system focused on collective healing through inner transformation and personal growth, using a variety of resources, even science; and focusing on CHA's official 12 steps to liberation.

Another highly relevant consideration is this: CHA can be used as a companion to any 12-step or non-12-step program, healing and awakening modality like yoga, or counseling process you may be utilizing. Unlike programs that demand exclusivity, CHA embraces absolute inclusivity, recognizing that healing and growth can come from a variety of sources. This flexibility allows individuals to integrate the CHA process with their existing practices without conflict, enhancing their overall journey; which easily supports and complements other methods by offering an additional layer of depth and understanding. By not mandating exclusivity, and also providing the option to establish your own steps, CHA empowers individuals to create a personalized and holistic trajectory to their healing and awakening. This approach naturally nurtures a more comprehensive and fulfilling path to self-discovery, while connecting with a community of like-minded friends steeped in collective wisdom. Other available resources, references and literature may be found at the CHA's official website: www.DiscoverCHA.org.

APPENDIX III

Foundational Themes of CHA

It's Okay

This reassures you that whatever you're feeling or going through is acceptable and neither makes you a good nor bad person. "It's okay" is an acknowledgement that everyone faces challenges, and it's perfectly natural to seek out help and humbly receive support, unconditionally.

You are not Alone

This reminds you there are others who have experienced similar struggles, and somehow opens the door to dissolving the idea of disconnection holding us back from coming out of our shell and truly blossoming.

We are Here for You

This underscores the healing power of a support system. It means that there are people who will not judge or condemn you, who genuinely care about your well-being, and are unconditionally willing to assist you on your journey. You do not have to face your struggles in isolation.

There is Another Way to Be Alive

This offers inspirational and life-liberating energy and possibility there are alternative paths to living a fulfilling and meaningful life beyond our habits, routines, and beliefs no longer serving us. It encourages you to explore new possibilities and creativity beyond your current struggles.

You Have Choices

This empowers you by reminding us that we have the agency and power to make decisions about our lives. You wield the power of choice to consciously choose healthier and more constructive paths; recognizing you are NOT bound by your past choices, beliefs, feelings, and behaviors.

You Are Allowed

This is about giving ourselves permission to think, feel, and express ourselves beyond our critical inner voices. We are allowed to have the experience we are having right here now, without trying to mentally change it or judge it. You are allowed to be exactly as you already are. Perfectly whole.

You are Already Whole, Worthy, Innocent, Complete, Enough

This highlights your everlasting, natural, and intrinsic innocence, worthiness and completeness. It signifies that you do not need external validation or to modify your behavior or use substances to feel whole. You are already complete, loveable, enough, just as you are; always! Even when acting out addictions.

APPENDIX IV

The 12 Steps of Collective Healing Anonymous

1. We humbly acknowledge the impact of [the coping mechanism dependency] on our lives, understanding it is only temporary, and embrace the powers within us to reclaim autonomy of our minds.

2. We opened to the possibility that the power to restore conscious clarity resides within ourselves, and that we can utilize this Universal Loving Force and inner strength as Trust, Compassion, Gratitude, Diligent Focus, and Willingness, while utilizing relevant external guidance and support whenever we so choose.

3. Made a conscious decision to turn to and trust the deeper and silent wisdom and Universal Loving Intelligence within, choosing to rely on this inner guidance rather than being driven solely by our conditioning, mental will, thoughts, obsessions, and compulsions. By embracing this inner wisdom, our false identities gradually dissolve as awareness of our essential, already whole, inseparable being emerges.

4. By acknowledging our primal innocence, we made a compassionate and fearlessly honest inventory of self judgments we have been carrying in the mind.

5. Admitted to our Universal Self, our personal self, and to another human being the exact nature of our believed self judgments. (Hint: All three are one in the same.)

6. Were entirely ready to free ourselves from ALL self criticism, self judgment, self blame, guilt, and unworthiness by allowing ourselves to feel whatever we have been avoiding.

7. Humbly sought inwardly through meditative self-inquiry to compassionately observe and understand the innocent nature of our beliefs, behaviors, feelings, and suffering.

8. Made a list of all persons we believe we have harmed and became willing to make amends to them all.

9. Made direct amends to such people wherever possible, except when to do so would injure them, others, or myself.

10. Continued to remain mindful and alert to unnecessary inner dialogue and judgmental thoughts, as well as externalized speech and behaviors; and when we believed we caused harm, promptly admitted it.

11. Sought through meditation, self-inquiry, and various other Sacred Processes to fully understand and become aware of the nature of suffering, experience, divine reality, and mySELF; thereby completely dissolving the illusion of separation and unwholeness.

12. Having become deeply healed and awakened through the power of awareness, we continue allowing life to effortlessly flow with ease, balance, and grace, while our lives effortlessly unfold beyond personal identity and both the illusion of control and separation.

APPENDIX V

The Essence of the Peace President Collection of Books

A Collection of Books as Guidance toward Inner Transformation, Conscious Government, and Peaceful Coexistence

[Please note that this book, "Life beyond Death: The Ego's Journey of Being Human" is NOT part of the Peace President Collection.]

For decades to centuries to millennia past, human beings have been struggling with one another, fighting, blaming—arguing over who is right or wrong, good or bad. Governments and civilizations continue rising and falling while unnecessary social divides and war persist. Regardless of the era, whether played out in ancient to medieval times or modern day, conflict appears to be arising from one set of beliefs and identities versus another set of beliefs and identities; as if there are two or more sets of rigid opinions in opposition to each other, always.

Could it be that we are often unaware of solutions to our challenges because we were born into cultures defined by divisive identities and conflicting traditions—cultures that treat these self-generated divisions as socially acceptable? We may simply not know any better, and relying solely on the limited perceptions we have been taught to trust. Perhaps we have yet to question the true validity of those beliefs and assumptions. For instance, why are there two political parties always divided instead of one unified party that is all inclusive? One nation, undivided? A genuinely United States?

An Intimate and Personal Story

I recall feeling so deeply depressed, constrained, and frozen, as if living life was more like being caught in an amusement park of suffering, where I was living the same day over and over—like the movie 'Groundhog's Day'—lost in a day of tension, stress, anxiety—always in search of finding pleasant sensations while avoiding unpleasant feelings. Apparently, I thought, and believed, I was happy, yet discovered 'my' happiness was conditional—greatly limited—limiting the reality of unconditional joyous peace always present underneath whatever appears to be happening. Little did I know this was happening: I was becoming accustomed to avoiding feeling while a type of numbness was accumulating; specifically due to living in a socially accepted survival mode of self-preservation deemed 'normal' by practically everyone! In other words, I was unconsciously lost trying and striving to become someone or something I was not, trying to appease others, and fit into a world and society which seemed to be going in the wrong direction.

You see, I was born into a beautifully creative, loving, and wonderful world, yet highly destructive. A world of human consciousness where war, violence, greed, and learning to deny my experience and intuition was the cultural norm; which is to say: For most of my life, I was unaware that my self-defeating programming and conditioning being acted out as unconscious reactions and self-defeating compulsions were dictating my life. I was completely unaware or in denial of this: that I had been manipulating my mind to adapt to a profoundly sick society, because that is what everyone said to do! Basically, I was going with the crowd of self-destructive cultural patterns that were socially acceptable, instead of questioning the legitimacy of them. In other words, it seemed easier, somehow, to live in denial, than confront what was really happening; even though the cultural, personal, and family patterns I had been relying on to provide a sense of security, self worth, and happiness, were deeply unsettling, and only temporarily fulfilling at best.

The Profound Possibility

Of course, the society or world, as human collective consciousness in which I was born, wields absolute potential to transcend any and ALL self-defeating personal, societal, national, global, and generational thought habits, behavioral patterns, and mind-made divisions. Yet, that insight or realization did not arise until much later in life, when somehow, I became aware of this: that what I had been trained and taught to believe would bring everlasting fulfillment, peace, joy, and prosperity, was never going to work. (The keyword there is everlasting.) So, obviously, there was great confusion, self-judgment and hatred that developed, and ongoing apathy for the world, and learned self-oppression resulting from trying to fit into social patterns and concepts that simply "don't work." A big part of the belief system of self-contempt that developed was due to this: believing I was a failure or not good enough because the happiness promised by trusting what I had been conditioned to believe would bring everlasting feelings of worthiness and wholeness never proved to be true. So, of course, no matter how hard I attempted to 'follow the rules' and advice programmed and conditioned into my mind over the years, it never brought forth what was promised; no matter what I did, said, thought, believed, or identified with. What a wildly amazing moment of conscious clarity—to acknowledge the possibility that virtually everything I was told about living a life of happiness, joy, peace, and prosperity—was utterly untrue, in reality.

However, despite the tremendous inner turmoil building throughout my life and denying sacred wisdom deep within my being, I somehow always knew in my heart that a life free of suffering, unworthiness, division, violence, and fear, was possible; a truer life not only in and as myself, but a truer possibility for Humanity as a whole. At the time, I had not yet become aware there is a choice, a profoundly conscious choice each and every one of us can acknowledge: To choose self-destructive patterns, victimhood, and denial—OR—productive life liberating sacred processes and sacred human qualities toward inner wellbeing, unimaginable joy, and profound conscious clarity.

Through what I refer to as Sacred Processes of Awakening like meditation, this awareness illuminated itself: Every human being on the planet is capable of waking up to the truth of us—our most compassionate and loving and generous nature, absent of the illusion of separation, and free of our innocently self-destructive tendencies. We need only willingly open, somehow, to those possibilities amid our resistance and compulsions to avoid what we know in our hearts to be true. Perhaps, by embracing the healing and life liberating powers of humility and forgiveness. Somehow when one wholeheartedly becomes interested in the most sacred qualities like humility and forgiveness and patience, we begin acknowledging there is another way to live. We also begin opening to possibilities beyond our wildest dreams, like this: that we can free ourselves from self-judgment permanently, heal unattended sorrow forever, and come out of hiding, whenever we so choose.

Could it be we continue venturing down our generational paths of suffering as anxiety, ill content, blame, worry, stress, and division, because we are adverse to possibilities that may require radical self-honesty and inner transformation? Could our self sustained power struggles, misery, greed, and violence be asking for conscious clarity and peaceful and compassionate understanding, versus the unhelpful mental strategy of accusing, criticizing, blaming, and judging ourselves that sustain the confusion, despair, unworthiness, divisions, conflict, and rigid viewpoints—both individually and collectively? Let us not fret. There is a choice in the matter. There is Good News! This is another way to be, alive!

Opening unto Feeling, Healing, Awakening

By inspiring us to partake in Sacred Processes toward inner liberation, conscious government, and peaceful coexistence, the essence of the Peace President Collection of Books and Peace President United is this: To invite and embrace healing, feeling, and awakening unto the loving truth of us, by willingly opening to new possibilities for ourselves, our nation, government, and humanity as a whole, beyond our socially acceptable divisive beliefs and identities, painful habits, and self-destructive trends.

Practically speaking: Although, as Humanity, as citizens of countries and respective governments, who harness the most amazing potential and life liberating qualities capable of enhancing wellbeing, and providing vital necessities and basic human needs to everyone on earth, we appear to be innocently asleep, suffering, confused, unconscious, and mostly unaware of our individual and collective self-destructive, neglectful, and divisive momentum; as well as our most loving and greatest possibilities! In other words, we are unaware of our absolutely amazing and loving all inclusive potential, because our attention seems to be focused elsewhere!

We appear to be innocently lost in the grip of judgment and greed, and blaming anyone and ourselves while rationalizing and justifying those divisive and hurtful energies—regardless if those thoughts and actions are destructive and sustain unnecessary turmoil, violence, unworthiness, and separation. Remember, there is

Good News! There exists the absolute possibility to Coexist Peacefully beyond blame, hatred, suffering, division, and destruction; that is, when we open our hearts and minds to new possibilities, the truth of ourselves, and Universal Vision.

Perhaps, amid our resistance to genuinely and willingly acknowledging our greatest all inclusive and loving potential, we must first welcome self-forgiveness and the infinite grace of gratitude, mercy, and abundance.

There is Good News! Are you open to the possibilities? Have we finally had enough of the old ideas and habits leading us down a path of destruction, disconnection, division, confusion, despair, and violence? Have we had enough of denying ourselves our most loving and all inclusive sacred qualities such as compassion and humility? Isn't it time for foundational changes and transformation in our individual lives and as a nation to unfold in the most loving and unifying manner; even if those essential shifts may be uncomfortable and unsettling for a little while?

The "Peace President Collection" of books offers awareness and poignant suggestions, guidance, and solutions to our individual yearning for inner peace and collective calling for positive change beyond division and conflict. These works acknowledge the urgency of embracing new possibilities and transcending old patterns that have led us astray—patterns of division, confusion, blame, and violence. Through Sacred Processes and by embracing our most Sacred Human Qualities, like compassion and humility, this wisdom is calling for foundational changes and transformation, both individually and as a nation; and world.

The Peace President Collection reminds us that while such shifts may be uncomfortable initially, they hold the promise of a more loving, unified, and peaceful future, not only for ourselves, but most importantly, for future generations. It is an invitation to seize the opportunity for lasting change and to consciously choose the path of feeling, healing, and awakening.

With Timeless Love,

Peace President

www.peacepresidentunited.org

www.ingramcontent.com/pod-product-compliance
Lightning Source LLC
Chambersburg PA
CBHW071929290426
44110CB00013B/1530